OPERATION REDWOOD

Operation Redwood

Published by The Conrad Press in the United Kingdom 2020

Tel: +44(0)1227 472 874
www.theconradpress.com
info@theconradpress.com

ISBN 978-1-914913-92-1

Copyright © Mick Battley and Pete Lattanzi 2022

The moral right of Mick Battley and Pete Lattanzi to be identified as authors of this work has been asserted in accordance with the Copyright, Designs and Patents Act 1988.

All rights reserved.

Typesetting and Cover Design by: Charlotte Mouncey, www.bookstyle.co.uk

The Conrad Press logo was designed by Maria Priestley.

Printed and bound in Great Britain by Clays Ltd, Elcograf S.p.A.

OPERATION REDWOOD

AN ORIGINAL SCREENPLAY
BY MICK BATTLEY AND PETE LATTANZI

FADE IN:

FULL SHOT - NORTH EAST COAST OF IRELAND - MORNING

A large British Coast Guard vessel cuts through the waves in the Irish Sea. It rolls through the weakening seas of a recent storm, spray driving over the bow as it parallels the coast. Radio traffic is heard in the background. CAPTAIN SWANSON and Executive Officer MR. NASH are on the bridge, both looking through binoculars. The Captain spots a forty-foot steel-hulled fishing vessel that has crashed on the rocks.

SWANSON

There she is. About fifteen degrees off the port bow. Mr Nash, can you prepare a search crew?

NASH

Right away, sir.

NASH picks up the ship telephone.

NASH

Bridge here. Prepare a launch, take a four-man party. Standby for launch orders and give us a radio check when you're underway.

VOICE

(through the phone) Aye aye sir.

NASH hangs up the phone.

SWANSON

What's our depth?

NASH looks at the depth gauge.

> NASH
>
> We're holding at twenty-one fathoms sir.

> SWANSON
>
> Very good. Take us in to 150 yards off the shore, idle speed, watch your depth, then make ready to drop anchor. Those poor guys. It must have been a rough ride in that gale.

> NASH
>
> Yes sir.

CUT TO:

EXT. STERN OF SHIP - MORNING

A launch with crew, led by CHIEF CLARKE, is lowered into the water and heads into the wind, toward the wreck about one hundred yards away.

> CLARKE
>
> Radio check. Radio check. HMS Essex, launch is underway.

CUT TO:

FULL SHOT LAUNCH APPROACHING WRECK ON THE ROCKS - MORNING

The launch runs up on the beach between large boulders. The crew gets out and struggles over rocks to the fishing vessel. The crew, including STAN, climbs up the side of the vessel onto the deck, cautiously looking around.

> CLARKE
>
> You two take a look down below.
> Stan let's check out the wheelhouse.

Two sailors climb down a ladder into the dimly lit hold.
Clarke and Stan walk into the wheelhouse and look around.
Clarke picks up the radio.

> CLARKE
>
> HMS Essex, search crew is on board. The wheelhouse is
> empty. It appears to have been cleaned out.

> SWANSON'S VOICE
>
> (through the radio) What do you mean cleaned out?

> CLARKE'S VOICE
>
> All the radio equipment, charts and navigation....

> SAILOR
>
> Chief! Chief! You need to come down here right away!

> CHIEF
>
> Ah, stand by Essex.

Clarke turns to the sailor, who is out of breath.

> CHIEF
>
> What have you got?

                            SAILOR

Chief, the ship's loaded with weapons. Everything's in
crates. Rifles, crates of ammunition and it looks like
packaged military explosives. You'd better come take a
look.

The three men run across the deck and climb down the ladder.

                                                    CUT TO:

INT. BELOW DECK HOLD - MORNING
*The search crew stands at the bottom of the ladder in a foot of
water, surrounded by crates of weapons, ammunition, explosives
and boxes marked detonators.*

                            CHIEF

Holy Christ! We need to get off the ship. Don't use
your radios or we'll all get blown to kingdom come.
Come on lads, right away now.

*The crew jumps off the side of the vessel onto the rocks and run up
to the top of the beach.*

                                                    CUT TO:

EXT. TOP OF BEACH - MORNING
Clarke, out of breath, picks up the portable radio.

                            CHIEF

HMS Essex over!

                            NASH

(through the radio) Essex, go ahead.

                            CHIEF
          Yes sir, can you go to secure voice?

                                                         CUT TO:
_____

INT. BRIDGE OF THE ESSEX - MORNING
*SWANSON, irritated, looks over at XO Nash. Nash reaches up
and switches the radio to voice privacy.*

                          SWANSON
          Go ahead now, what is it?

                       CLARKE'S VOICE
          (through the radio) Captain, the vessel is abandoned
          and appears to contain a very large load of military
          weapons, ammunition, explosives and detonators. It is
          taking on water at this time. Please advise.

*Swanson, looking surprised, faces Nash and speaks into the
microphone.*

                          SWANSON
          Send back the launch for a security detail. Hold your
          position. We'll be out shortly. Confirm, did you say it is
          abandoned?

                       CLARKE'S VOICE
          (through the radio) Affirmative sir. No one on board.

Nash nods to the Captain and turns, running towards the stairs.

NASH

I'll make the call to Command Captain. Do we have a name?

SWANSON

Chief, do we have a name for the ship?

CLARKE'S VOICE

(through the radio)
No sir, no name. No flag. It appears to be a stateless...

CUT TO:

INT. BRIDGE OF THE ESSEX - MORNING

The interior of the bridge flashes in a blinding white light. Two seconds later a large concussion blows in several windows, allowing the roar of the explosion to enter, knocking both men to the floor. An alarm sounds in the background.

DISSOLVE TO:

INT. INN ON THE PARK RESTAURANT, LONDON - EVENING

Two wine glasses are being filled with a blood red Merlot. A trickle of wine runs over one glass, pooling into the white linen tablecloth. Classical music plays softly in the four-star restaurant. Two men in business suits are sitting across from each other at a table at the window overlooking the park. STEVE YOUNG, in his thirties, is stocky, rough looking, has a ponytail and speaks with an English East End accent. OMAR COR, fifty, is American, short, bald and overweight. His hair is trimmed very smart. He wears a pinkie ring and his fingers are manicured. Both men raise their glasses and tap them together.

STEVE

Thanks for coming, Omar. I appreciate you're a busy man.

OMAR

Not a problem Steve. I had business here in London anyway.

Steve opens a London Times newspaper on the table. It shows the headline of a ship explosion off the Irish coast, listing several casualties.

STEVE

I saw it in the news. That mess must have cost you a few bob.

Omar glances at the paper and continues eating.

OMAR

Shit happens, Steve. So why are you buying me this meal?

STEVE

Well the way I see it, I can move up to the top of your list if you're still able to supply those goods.

OMAR

I'm still in business. Who is your client?

STEVE

Just like every other client. Someone with a very urgent need.

CUT TO:

EXT. INN ON THE PARK RESTAURANT, LONDON - EVENING

A work van is parked with its lights out in an adjacent alley.

CUT TO:

INT. SURVEILLANCE VAN - EVENING

The interior of the van is packed with electronics and monitors. Quiet conversation is heard over speakers. ROBIN ERWIN, short and diminutive, is sitting in front of a monitor, watching intently. MICK BEECRAFT is sitting at a small desk in the back, reading the Sun newspaper, drinking coffee. Mick, 35, is average build with collar length hair. He is wearing a leather jacket.

ROBIN

He's slid a piece of paper over. I think it's going well.

Bored, Mick continues reading the newspaper.

MICK

Just film the fucking meet. I'll tell you if it's going well or not. You know, those wankers can fuck off in a second.

Mick puts the paper down and looks around the van.

MICK

All of your gear working? You got enough of it? In the

old days I'd be sitting at the next table, taking notes on a napkin.

ROBIN

Was that before or after they invented the wheel?

MICK

Oh get lost you cheeky sod! Just make sure you record it all. I've got a briefing with the guv'nor tomorrow and I want it to go well.

CUT TO:

INT. INN ON THE PARK RESTAURANT, LONDON - EVENING Omar and Steve continue eating and drinking.

STEVE

So what do you think? Yes or no?

Omar chews with his mouth open.

OMAR

It can be done.

Omar takes a sip of wine, slurping.

OMAR

Off the top of my head, it's going to run you about a million though.

STEVE

And you can deliver anywhere.

Omar wipes his mouth with a napkin.

OMAR

Within reason, Steven.

Both men rise from the table. Steve peels off several large pound notes and lays them on the table.

OMAR

I'll meet you here Thursday. Nine p.m. alright? I should have a better figure for you.

Omar hands the paper back to Steve who refuses it.

STEVE

You hang onto that so you get the order right.

Both men shake hands and turn towards the exit.

CUT TO:

INT. SURVEILLANCE VAN - EVENING
Robin turns around to Mick.

ROBIN

The meeting's over. They're leaving. Gonna meet again Thursday.

MICK

Are they now? Did the pony tail arrange that?

ROBIN

No. The fat one. And ponytail agreed.

MICK

OK. Did you get it all? I want this job to get the go
ahead. We ain't had a result in a while.

CUT TO:

EXT. INN ON THE PARK RESTAURANT, LONDON - EVENING
Omar and Steve are standing outside the entrance by the door man.
Steve pats Omar on the back. Steve gets into a black taxi and drives
off. Omar looks around nervously and walks back into the hotel.

CUT TO:

EXT. U.S. EMBASSY LONDON - MORNING
Mick runs up the stairs to the entrance, leather satchel in hand,
he holds open the door to let a lady in. He walks in behind her.

CUT TO:

INT. U.S. EMBASSY LONDON - MORNING
Mick walks up to the visitor desk. SEVERAL VERY LARGE U.S.
MARINES are standing behind it. Mick hands his credentials to
one of the marines who inspects it.

MICK

I'm here to see ROSEN please.
The marine picks up a phone and dials a number.

MARINE

Yes ma'am. A Metropolitan Police Sergeant Mick
Beecraft to see Mr. Rosen. Yes ma'am.

The marine hangs up the phone and hands Mick a visitor pass.

> MARINE
> Fourth floor sir. Room four twenty.

CUT TO:

INT. U.S. CUSTOMS ATTACHÉ OFFICE - MORNING

A SECRETARY walks Mick over to an interior office door and knocks on it. A voice answers to come in. The secretary opens the door for Mick and he thanks her as he enters and she closes the door behind him. Customs Attaché JERRY ROSEN walks around his desk to Mick and they shake hands.

> ROSEN
> Mick, nice to meet you finally.

> MICK
> Thanks for seeing me on such a short notice.

> ROSEN
> My pleasure. What do you have?
> Another wayward American I'll bet.

> MICK
> It appears so.

Mick hands Jerry a file marked 'CONFIDENTIAL' with surveillance photos of Omar. Jerry looks at the photos.

> MICK
> We have one tentatively identified as Omar Cor.

He claims to be an arms dealer looking to do some unlicensed business. He's staying at the Inn on the Park through Thursday.

ROSEN

Outstanding. Let me see what I can come up with for you.

CUT TO:

INT. NEW SCOTLAND YARD LOBBY - MORNING

Mick enters the crowded lobby of New Scotland Yard, satchel in hand, walking up to the uniformed officer behind the reception desk. He flashes his credentials.

MICK

Morning. Can you ring BANKS' secretary and let her know I'm in reception? I have a meeting with Mr. Banks at eleven.

UNIFORMED OFFICER

You can call yourself on the middle phone. Extension 3574.

MICK

Thanks.

Mick picks up the phone and dials the number.

CAROL'S VOICE

(through the phone) Good morning.

CAROL'S VOICE

Detective Chief Inspector Banks office. How may I help you?

Mick scans the lobby, looking at everyone passing by.

MICK

Very posh, Carol. It's Mick here. Is Nick in?

CUT TO:

INT. CAROL AT HER DESK - MORNING

CAROL

No, he's running late. He said to tell you to wait in the canteen and he will join you there as soon as he's hung up his coat. How are you Mick? Long time no hear. You still married or seeing that WPC at Ilford?

CUT TO:

INT. NEW SCOTLAND YARD LOBBY - MORNING

Mick talking on the phone.

MICK

Divorced. Thanks for asking. And the WPC gave up on me, so I'm foot loose if you fancy a drink.

CAROL'S VOICE

(through the phone) Wait till Christmas.
(laughing) I'll tell the boss you're in the canteen.

CUT TO:

INT. CAROL AT HER DESK - MORNING

Carol hangs up the phone and turns her head to the open office door behind her.

CAROL

Mick's waiting down in the canteen.

BANKS VOICE

He can wait. What's the next operation name available Carol?

Carol reaches down and unlocks a drawer. pulls out a file, opens it and looks.

CAROL

REDWOOD sir.

She opens the drawer,

BANKS VOICE

Save that for me would you? If I approve his plan we'll give him that one.

CUT TO:

INT. CANTEEN - MORNING

Mick is sitting alone at a corner table by a window, staring down into the street below, coffee cup in hand, lost in his thoughts. BANKS, in his fifties with grey hair, wearing slacks and a sweater, walks up behind him.

                          BANKS

Morning Mick. Coffee?

                           MICK

No thanks Guv. I'm OK.

                          BANKS

So what you got for me then?

                           MICK

I think we have a live one boss. We have what I think is
a U.S. arms dealer trying to drum up business. I've got
video of the meeting if you want to watch.

BANKS stands up.

                          BANKS

Come on then. Let's go to the briefing room.

                                                    CUT TO:

INT. OFFICE HALLWAY - MORNING
*DCI BANKS and Mick walk up to a set of double doors marked
'BRIEFING ROOM'. Mick opens the right door for BANKS.*

                                                    CUT TO:

INT. BRIEFING ROOM - MORNING
*BANKS walks to the front of the room as Mick turns on the lights
then dims them down. Mick walks past DCI BANKS, seated two
rows back from a large screen and places a tape into a VCR.*

CUT TO:

INT. BRIEFING ROOM - MORNING

The large screen lights up BANKS' face as he squints and puts on glasses. Mick sits in the shadows. Audio of the conversation is heard in the background. Moments pass as Banks looks up at the screen.

BANKS

Looks promising. Did you call the U.S. officials yet?

MICK

Yep. Stopped off on the way over here and met with the Customs Attaché.
He has a copy of the tape. He's checking on the American.

BANKS

And what about the other one there?

MICK

He's your typical pain in the arse villain type. I'd like to make him go away after this is all over.

BANKS

I bet you would. I don't have to tell you Mick, if I give the go ahead for this job, there has to be no fuck ups. Do you know what I'm saying son? I'm retiring soon and I won't be around to fight in your corner.

MICK

Nick, I know. I appreciate what you've done for me but

I think this has got legs. We can take it the whole way.

Banks looks skeptically at Mick and without looking, picks up the phone next to him and dials an extension.

> BANKS
>
> Carol. Banks here. What was the name of that operation again?

Banks writes on a piece of paper.

> BANKS
>
> Yep. Got it.

Banks hands Mick the slip of paper. Mick looks at the paper.

> MICK
>
> Redwood.

Banks stands up and walks towards the door.

> BANKS
>
> You run everything through me you understand? Cover the next meet, then I'll pull up a meeting with Detective Superintendent Morrison. If that goes well, then we can approve overseas travel and keep our hands on the job.

Banks opens the door and turns to Mick.

> BANKS
>
> Don't want those Yanks getting all the glory, right?

> MICK
>
> Thanks Nick. Gov. We'll get the results. Promise.

Mick takes the video out of the machine and turns to DCI Banks.

BANKS

Good luck mate. We'll have a drink when it's all over.

Banks closes the door. Mick picks up the phone and dials a number. A voice answers.

MICK

Robin. Operation Redwood. Mark it up, get the van in order and tell the rest we got the go ahead.

Mick hangs up and walks out of the briefing room.

CUT TO:

INT. MICK IN CAR - EVENING

Mick is driving through the streets of London. A light rain is falling. The windshield wipers are on. Night is starting to fall. Mick's cell phone rings. He reaches for it and answers it.

MICK

Hello?

ROSEN'S VOICE

(through the phone) Mick, its Rosen. You have a minute?

MICK

Yes sir.

ROSEN'S VOICE

(through the phone) Mick, I have some information on your boy from the restaurant. We also have him identified as Omar Cor. You were right, he's a borderline American ex-patriot who lists himself as an export broker. Ships everything through third party companies though. He's also claimed Swiss and, hold on, Costa Rican citizenship.

MICK

He can do that?

ROSEN'S VOICE

(through the phone) Sure. All it takes is money. You want to get together and talk?

MICK

Absolutely. Can I call you in a few days?

ROSEN'S VOICE

(through the phone) You bet. I'll wait to hear from you.

CUT TO:

INT. SURVEILLANCE VAN OUTSIDE INN ON THE PARK - EVENING

Mick takes a seat inside the van, closing the sliding door next to him. TV monitors light up Robin's face.

MICK

How's it going? All the players here?

ROBIN

Well pony tail got here early. Fat man just showed up.

They're sitting at the same table.

Robin hands Mick the headphones.

ROBIN

Have a listen. You can watch on monitor two but please don't touch anything.

MICK

OK. OK.

Mick puts on the headphones.

MICK

Right, I can hear them. You did bring some coffee didn't you?

Robin sighs, hands a thermos to Mick.   Mick pours a cup and places the cup on top of the monitor. Robin carefully removes the cup and sighs again.

ROBIN

Fucking detectives never understand liquids and electrics don't mix.

Mick sees Robin's lips moving and the cup being taken away.

MICK

What you saying? Where you going with that?

Mick takes the cup and holds it, swearing at Robin.

CUT TO:

INT. INN ON THE PARK RESTAURANT, LONDON – EVENING

Omar Cor and Steve are sitting at the table over drinks.

> STEVE
>
> So my friend. Where do we stand?

> OMAR
>
> I can definitely get the order. I can ship it to Africa listed as computers and re-route it. All you have to do is meet it when it arrives at your destination.

> STEVE
>
> I'll give you that later when I know the ship has left. I can tell you, it's going to be somewhere in England.

> OMAR
>
> OK. I'll square away the licenses and shipping documents.

> STEVE
>
> And the cost of all this good will?

Omar opens his cell phone, enters some numbers and shows it to Steve then closes the phone.

> STEVE
>
> Seven hundred fifty thousand.
> All right.

CUT TO:

INT. SURVEILLANCE VAN OUTSIDE INN ON THE PARK - EVENING
Robin turns around to Mick and shakes his head in disbelief.

MICK
You getting all this?

ROBIN
No. I'm taping the BBC. What do you think?

MICK
I think you're a mouthy little shit who should respect his Sergeant. I'll take that as a yes then.

Robin nods while looking back at the monitor, giggling.

CUT TO:

INT. INN ON THE PARK RESTAURANT, LONDON - EVENING
Omar and Steve push their chairs back from the table. Omar slurps the last of his drink as they stand.

STEVE
Well that's it then. I'll call you in a couple of days.

OMAR
So when do I meet your client?

STEVE
Soon enough my friend.

They shake hands. Steve throws pound notes on the table. They walk together to the elevator.

CUT TO:

EXT. INN ON THE PARK RESTAURANT, LONDON - EVENING
Omar and Steve shake hands again. Omar enters a waiting cab and leaves. Steve watches the cab drive off, pulls the collar of his coat up and begins to walk the opposite direction down the street. He stops and stares at the surveillance van, looks around, then reaches into his coat pocket as he walks towards the van.

CUT TO:

INT. SURVEILLANCE VAN OUTSIDE INN ON THE PARK - EVENING
Mick is talking on a cell phone.

MICK
Yep Gov. It's set up. I'll tell you more once I've...

The side door to the van flies open and Steve jumps in, on top of Mick, slamming it behind him. Mick, talking on the phone, jumps up out of his seat, swearing, spilling coffee everywhere. Robin turns around and screams. Mick grabs Steve with his free hand and reaches back to hit him, then stops.

MICK
You complete fucking idiot!

Mick speaks into the phone.

MICK
No, not you guv. That fucking undercover detective muppet I work with just jumped us in the van.

Sometimes I wonder who's side he's on. No guv. I'm joking, he's fine. I'll have a chat with him and see you tomorrow at the Yard with the final details. Cheers boss.

Mick hangs up and looks at Steve, who's smiling.

                    MICK

You happy? You believe this guy? Be honest Steve, I ain't paying for no more jollies.

                    STEVE

Mick, I believe him. You can see it in his little beady eyes. He's a greedy little fuck who wants that money. I reckon this is the one we've been waiting for.

Mick looks over at Robin who nods in agreement. They all smile and shake hands.

                    ROBIN

Maybe next time you'll lock the door.

                                                        CUT TO:

INT. AUSTIN TEXAS GYM - MORNING

Sitting alone on a bench in a crowded gym is a man with his back to the crowd. PETE VELLETRI is thin but athletic. In the noise and background music, he is leaning forward, sweat dripping off his chin, doing isolated curls. A cell phone rings, he puts down the dumbbell and reaches forward for a cell phone, revealing the fresh scar of a bullet wound below his shoulder blade.

                              PETE

Hello?

                      SUPERVISOR REAGAN'S VOICE

(through the phone) Hey do you still work here? What's
that music? Are you in a bar?

                              PETE

No sir, I'm almost done working out. Do you need me
somewhere?

                      SUPERVISOR REAGAN'S VOICE

(through the phone) Yeah, get moving and get to the
office. The boss wants to see us.

                              PETE

Sure thing. Fifteen minutes?

                      SUPERVISOR REAGAN'S VOICE

(through the phone) Go.

                                                    CUT TO:

INT. OFFICE HALLWAY IN FRONT OF ELEVATORS - DAY

*Pete walks down a hallway tucking in his dress shirt. He folds his
shirt over a gun butt tucked under his belt. He runs his fingers
through his wet hair. He passes a sign on the wall with a U.S.
Customs seal and title: U.S. Customs Service -Resident Agent in
Charge - Austin Texas. He nods to passing agents. He enters the
door opposite the hallway.*

CUT TO:

INT. RESIDENT AGENT IN CHARGE OFFICE - DAY
RESIDENT AGENT IN CHARGE MYLES PORTER, a chain smoking, heavy-set man, is sitting at his desk, awards and memorabilia line the office, Group Supervisor JAMES REAGAN, short and balding, is sitting in a chair in front of the desk. Pete enters the room.
PORTER looks at his watch.

> PORTER
>
> Come on in.   Take a seat.

> PETE
>
> Thank you.

> REAGAN
>
> We got a call this morning from our Attaché, London. The Brits are working on an arms case involving an American with a local company.

Reagan hands Pete a file.
Pete opens the file and flips through the paperwork.

> REAGAN
>
> I want you to open a case and start the preliminary work. Go take a look at the business.

Reagan points to the file.

> REAGAN
>
> The Attaché said the Brits are negotiating with this guy for a container full of military grade weapons. He's

got a shipping company here in Austin. They have an undercover into him right now and think they can introduce one of our U/Cs into the case. Make a call to them when you're finished going over that.

PETE

The Attaché?

REAGAN

No, the Brits. Get a hold of their case agent, or whatever they call them over there, and get the rest of the details. His name is on the bottom of their report.

PETE

Yes sir.

PORTER

I don't need to tell you, however this case works out, I don't need headquarters or the embassy calling me bitching we screwed something up. Make sure you got all the I's dotted and T's crossed on this. Jerry's been working hard over there improving relations. Let's use this to further thing along. Right?

PETE

Yes sir.

REAGAN

Thanks Pete, I'll see you in the office in a minute.

Pete gets up and walks out.

                    REAGAN
So what kind of odds are they putting on this thing?

                    PORTER
Jerry sounded like it's a viable case. He said the
Metropolitan Police Regional Crime Squad is working
it. He thinks Scotland Yard wouldn't mess with it if it
didn't have potential. What about him?

                    REAGAN
He'll be all right. He's getting settled in from his
transfer. He worked mostly dope up north, but I know
he also worked on a couple of arms export cases. Just
finished a nasty divorce.

                    PORTER
She really shoot him?

                    REAGAN
That's the story.

                    PORTER
Well, tell him if he's looking for sympathy it's in the
dictionary.

                    REAGAN
Dictionary?

PORTER

Yeah. It's between shit and syphilis.

CUT TO:

EXT. INDUSTRIAL BUSINESS PARK - AFTERNOON

Pete and a female agent, DONNA, drive slowly down a business street looking for the shipping company address.

PETE

2101B Norfolk. It's gotta be around here somewhere.

DONNA

Tranquility Shipping. You gotta be kidding. Kinda has a perverted Zen thing going there. Go on by. It doesn't look like much. I'll get some pictures on the next pass.

Donna looks down at the camera, turning it on.

DONNA

Did you get a hold of the Brits?

Pete parks the car at the end of the street in view of the business.

PETE

I did. They sounded pretty excited about it. Man, they're a bitch to understand.

DONNA

What are you talking about?

PETE

I mean the accent.

DONNA

Accent?

PETE

Yeah.

DONNA

Have you listened to yourself lately? *You's, dems, dose.*
Screw this, screw that.
Talk about a New York accent. Fits in real well down
here too.

Pete smiles.

PETE

New York! I'm from Jersey. And 'asshole' is a greeting
where I come from, Miss Manners.

DONNA

Here comes somebody.

Omar walks out of the business front door, talking on a cell phone.
He locks the door. He gets into a Mercedes and drives off. Donna
takes several pictures.

PETE

That's him. You get it?

Donna starts taking pictures.

                    DONNA
Fucking A. You going to follow him?

Pete looks at Donna, feigning surprise.

                    PETE
Ahhh, no. We'll spot check him for now and get up on
him later.

                    DONNA
So what did the Brits have to say about this guy?

                    PETE
Their U/C met with him twice. They gave him what
they're calling a shopping list. There's enough arms and
explosives on it to overthrow the third world country of
your choice. Anyway, fat boy here didn't flinch when he
saw the list and says he can deliver.

                    DONNA
Did they talk price?

                    PETE
The bidding started at one million, not including tax,
title and destination.

Pause in the conversation.
Pete and Donna sit staring out the window.

                    DONNA
So what happens next?

                              PETE

They've been putting off talking to him until they got a
hold of us. The Attaché and headquarters opted us in,
so here we are. Their case agent's coming in Thursday.

                              DONNA

They're not wasting any time are they. Hey. I'll trade
you that money case of mine for this. I heard the Brit
looks like James Bond.

Pete starts the car.

                              PETE

Still trying to poach my cases. James Bond huh?
Probably more like Benny Hill. I'll pass.

                                               DISSOLVE TO:

INT. CONFERENCE ROOM RAC AUSTIN - AFTERNOON
REAGAN is seated at the head of the table. Department of
Commerce agent LEONARD FILLMORE, ATF Agent YOUNG and
Assistant U.S. Attorney RICHARD HANLEY are sitting next to him.
Secretary Cathy is sitting near the door. The door opens. Pete
walks in with Mick, introduces him to everyone. Everyone shakes
hands.

                             REAGAN

Cathy, can you tell Mr. Porter everyone is here?

                             CATHY

Certainly.

Cathy leaves. Reagan turns to Mick.

REAGAN

Take a seat Mick. How was your flight?

MICK

OK thank you. A little bumpy over Nova Scotia.

REAGAN

You all settled in at the hotel?

MICK

Yes sir. Thanks.

Reagan glances over Mick's shoulder to Pete who shrugs and raises his eyebrows as if he's not impressed. Cathy sticks her head into the room.

CATHY

Mr. Reagan, the RAC is on a conference call, he said to go ahead with the meeting.

REAGAN

Thanks Cathy. Take a seat. Well everyone knows why we're here. Mick, can I put you on the spot and tell us what you have to date?

Mick takes on a serious demeanour.

MICK

Certainly. Operation Redwood.

Mick opens a briefcase and hands out copies of a report to everyone.

MICK

I think everyone is current on the short history of this case. We have not spoken to the villain since our last meeting two weeks ago.

HANLEY looks across the table at Pete and silently mouths 'villain?' Pete smiles.

MICK

I have handed to you what we are referring to as the 'shopping list'. As you can see, it is quite a substantial amount of weapons and explosives.

ATF Special Agent WALTER YOUNG reads from the paper.

YOUNG

Three hundred and fifty M-16 machine guns. An equal number of Smith and Wesson 9mm pistols. Thirty cases,

He pauses and looks up.

YOUNG

Thirty cases? Fragmentation grenades. Five hundred cases of .223 ball ammunition. That's a lot of brass.

YOUNG

Two hundred kilos of C4 plastic explosives. Four boxes, fifty count each, electric detonators. Two Barrett fifty caliber sniper rifles. One thousand rounds fifty caliber ball ammunition. Fifteen forty millimetre grenade launchers...

YOUNG looks at Mick.

YOUNG

Your U/C gave this list to the target and he says he can produce and ship it?

MICK

Yes sir, in ninety days. He said there may be a delay with the explosives but he would get back with us.

YOUNG

Holy shit.

Mick looks at Young stone-faced.

REAGAN

Pete?

PETE

The target quoted this shipment at one million dollars, but the final price is still under negotiation. Mick's crew is eager to get one of our under-covers into the mix since so much of this is happening here.

REAGAN

Who did you have in mind?

PETE

I went through basic with an agent in Houston who'd be perfect if we can get him. His dad was in the Air Force stationed in England, this guy grew up over there.

He sounds like Mick Jagger.

                    REAGAN
Give him a call after this and see what his schedule is
like. What about the money?

                    PETE
We'll need to show fat man we have the funds before he
starts ordering.

                    REAGAN
Will the bank front us that kind of cash to an
undercover account?

                    PETE
I doubt it. Not without charging some serious points.
We can open a dummy account. I can order a wire
transfer from main treasury through headquarters.
That'll keep the banks out of it.
Pete, if you want, through one of our accounts, insulate

                    PETE

                    YOUNG
you can route it undercover it a little bit.
I'll take you up on that, thanks.

                    REAGAN
Len, what are the license requirements for this kind of
shipment?

LEONARD FILLMORE

Well for starters, he'd need licensing from the Department of State just for the firearms. Department of Defence would have to give a release to the supplier for the explosives, and grenades, depending on where they we're going. He would have to be pre- approved by DOD and Department of Transportation just to handle that kind of shipment. Prior to release, they would all contact us looking for any derogatory information. All in all, if he was legit, he would be looking at eighteen months just to get all the approvals.

REAGAN

Mick, it's our nickel, as we say.
We're going to want to take the load off here in the states. Will your people have a problem with that?

MICK

Oh no sir, not at all.

MICK

Since he has met with our people in the U.K. about this, he would be subject to prosecution in Crown Court on charges of conspiracy to import firearms. We would most certainly charge him when he gets out.

Reagan looks over at HANLEY.

HANLEY

Violation of the Arms Export Control Act, Neutrality Act, ITAR, conspiracy, smuggling. Sure, you can have him in about eighty years. What port do we think he will ship out of?

PETE

Probably Houston but they haven't said yet.

The door opens and the RAC enters.

PORTER

Sorry about that. So, we have everything worked out? We haven't started recalling our ambassadors yet have we? Ha ha.

No one laughs.

PETE

Mr. Porter, this is Metropolitan Police Detective Sergeant Michael Beecraft.

Mick stands. Shake hands.

MICK

How do you do.

PORTER

Fine thanks. They have you all squared away?

MICK

Sir?

PORTER

With the room and all.

MICK

Oh yes. Everything is fine.
We were just...

Porter interrupts.

PORTER

That's great. Make sure they take you out for some
barbecue while you're here. What's that place on fourth
street?

Porter turns to Mick.

PORTER

How long are you here for?

MICK

I'm leaving next...

Reagan interrupts.

REAGAN

We're done here, sir. Can I talk to you in your office?

*Everyone stands up. Reagan walks out of the room with Porter.
Mick leans toward Pete, speaking down towards the floor.*

MICK

Good to know we all have the same kind of governors.

Everyone laughs.

CUT TO:

EXT. CONFERENCE ROOM RAC AUSTIN - DAY
Pete and Mick walk out of the conference room.
Donna walks by and whispers to Pete.

DONNA

James Bond huh?

CUT TO:

INT. PETE'S PERSONAL CAR - DAY
Mick throws a small overnight bag in the trunk and gets in the car. Pete and Mick start driving to San Antonio for the weekend. Driving south on I-35, Pete puts a tape cassette in the player, both begin talking about their jobs, personal lives, starting to loosen up.

PETE

Finally. Man, I thought the weekend would never get here. How you doin' with the jet lag?

MICK

I'm making do. I really appreciate you taking me down to San Antonio. It is strange driving two hours just to go on the piss.

PETE

Yeah, Austin's mostly a college scene. There's no shortage of Senorita's where we're going.

MICK

You don't party much in Austin?

PETE

Hey, you don't shit where you eat.

Mick stares out the window smiling.
He thinks about the statement.

PETE

They have the Riverwalk, a couple of miles of
restaurants and bars. We'll have to check out the Alamo.

MICK

Your wife doesn't mind you going?

PETE

No. I don't think her boyfriend minds either.

MICK

Excuse me?

PETE

I'm divorced. How about you?

MICK

I'm in that club.
Costs a lot of money to join.

PETE

Amen to that.

CUT TO:

EXT. THE ALAMO - AFTERNOON SUNNY AND HOT

Mick and Pete are standing out in the Alamo front plaza, away from the crowds, facing the Alamo. Tourists are walking about, taking pictures.

> PETE
>
> Outnumbered six to one. Under siege by six thousand pissed off Mexicans for thirteen days. So they draw a line in the dirt asking anyone who wants to stay and fight to step over the line, knowing if they stayed they were gonna die.

> MICK
>
> Unbelievable.

> PETE
>
> Makes you wonder what you'd do if you were there.

Both stand for a minute, looking, not talking.

> PETE
>
> My people are looking close at this case. If anything goes wrong I'm gonna fade some bad heat.

Mick turns to Pete.

> MICK
>
> What are you saying?
> We don't know what we're doing?

Pete points his finger at Mick's chest.

PETE

I meant exactly what I said. Any mistakes here, any problems over there, the crooks get cold feet, somebody gets their fucking feelings hurt, it's gonna be on me and I gotta answer for it.

Mick moves into Pete's face.

MICK

What, you think you're alone there? I started this case and had to talk my governors into continuing on with it. On my own. They're keen on not making arses out of themselves in front of you bloody Yanks too. Your people aren't the only ones looking at budget balance sheets and arrest statistics you know. And don't forget, we invented drawing and quartering son.

MICK

They have plenty of cold wet places to send me if this doesn't go off, so you're not exactly on your own their mate.

There is a pause as they look at the Alamo.

PETE

How many of your guys did you lose here?

MICK

What? They said twelve English, nine Irish, four Scots.

PETE

Well we've just crossed the line in the dirt. Let's not

wind up like them. You ready for a drink?

Both turn and walk away from the Alamo.

> PETE
>
> Drawing and quartering. You guys still do that?

> MICK
>
> Oh mate, me governors live for it.

CUT TO:

EXT. MAD DOGS BRITISH PUB, RIVERWALK - EVENING

Mick and Pete are sitting at a table outside Mad Dogs Pub, both looking around at the people and buildings. Pete cuts the end of a cigar and lights it.

> PETE
>
> What do you think?

Mick points to the loft apartments overlooking the river.

> MICK
>
> Not half bad, I could happily live in one of those apartments.

> JODIE
>
> I do.

Mick turns to see Jodie standing behind him. She is slim with long brown hair.

MICK

Sorry?

JODIE

I do live in one of those. Sorry, I couldn't help but over hear you. You sound like you're from England.

MICK

Yep the East End.

JODIE

I've always wanted to go to London, you near there?

MICK

You work here and you've never been?

PETE

Here we go.

MICK

I'm only a couple of stops on the tube and you're there in the middle of London.

JODIE

Tube?

MICK

Sorry, the underground train, nice and quick.

Mick stands and introduces himself and Pete.

JODIE

I'm Jodie and I'm your waitress for the evening.

MICK

Nice.

Pete, sitting, taking a drag on his cigar, looks at Mick, smiles, and shakes his head.

PETE

That's great. Can we order now?

JODIE

Sure, what are you having.

MICK

Two Bud's and two Jameson's chasers.

JODIE

I'll bring them right over.

Jodie turns and walks towards the bar area, Mick looks back, noticing her short black skirt and legs.

MICK

I like the uniform.

Both men smile, Pete draws on his cigar.
Jodie returns with the drinks and places them on the table.

JODIE

Here you go, enjoy.

Jodie turns to walk away.

MICK

Excuse me. What time do you finish work, I'd like to get you a drink.

Jodie pauses, examining Mick.

JODIE

Ah, 10pm.

MICK

So you gonna let me buy you a drink? We're off tomorrow to see London bridge.

PETE

Oh no, not the London bridge story.

Mick and Pete laugh.

JODIE

What's the story?

MICK

I'll tell you at 10.

Jodie smiles and nod's her head.

JODIE

Ok.

MICK

Great I'll see you here?

Jodie walks away to the bar. Pete looks at Mick, draws on his cigar and exhales.

> PETE
>
> It'll end in tears. Always does.

Both men laugh, raise their Jameson's and drink a toast to a good job.

CUT TO:

EXT. MAD DOGS BRITISH PUB, RIVERWALK - EVENING
Mick is sitting alone at a table. Jodie approaches from behind, leans across Mick's shoulder.

> JODIE
>
> So now, the London Bridge story.

Mick stands and turns, he smiles, pulls a seat out for Jodie and they both sit. Jodie turns to the bar, raises her hand and points towards the table.

> MICK
>
> Hi ya, what can I get you to drink?

> JODIE
>
> It's done. I just ordered it, same as earlier.

> MICK
>
> Nice one, so how's you, long day?

> JODIE
>
> Same as normal...well what about London bridge?

Mick starts to tell the story.

CUT TO:

INT. HOTEL LOBBY PAY PHONE - EVENING

>   PETE
> Ok I'll tell him. We'll be leaving here in a couple of
> hours. We'll be
> back in Houston early tomorrow morning.

Pete writes on a paper.

>   PETE
> Ok go on, yeah, yeah, got that. Ok, see you tomorrow.

Pete hangs up and looks at the piece of paper.

>   PETE
> Nine a.m. British Airways to Heathrow.

>   PETE
> He'll love that.

EXT. MAD DOGS BRITISH PUB, RIVERWALK - EVENING
Mick finishing the London Bridge story.

>   MICK
> So there you go, I still need to find the little engraved
> heart..

>   JODIE
> That's so sweet!

MICK

Don't say that in front of Pete. He's just heard it on the way here and cringed. Talk of the devil. You OK mate?

Pete joins Mick and Jodie at the table.

PETE

That was the office. You're on the nine a.m. to London tomorrow morning out of Houston. The U/C and I will be over at the end of the week.

MICK

Bollocks.

JODIE

What do you two do?

PETE

(Sarcastically) Why yes Michael. What do you do?

MICK

Catch bad guys. I'm a Detective from Scotland Yard and Pete here works for his Uncle Sam.

Jodie looks at both men suspiciously.

JODIE

Don't tell me. You both left your badges in your other pants.

Mick turns to Pete. Pete pauses, then gives Mick his badge case. Mick gives Jodie both badge cases. Jodie examines them.

MICK

Don't worry, you're as safe as houses. Well that scuppers
our plans. When
do we leave?

PETE

As soon as we finish here.
I'll get
the car.

JODIE

Well hang on, I need a photo of you
guys!

*Jodie gets up, hands back the badges and walks off to the bar,
returning with a Polaroid camera and two Kilts.*

PETE

What the hell is she...?   Oh this doesn't look good.

JODIE

We're having a Scottish theme night next week so
we've got some kilts in and you two will be the first
photographed in them.

*Mick and Pete smile, put the kilts on at the table, drop their jeans
to their ankles, put on dark sunglasses.*

JODIE

Nicely done.

Jodie calls a member of the staff over to take a photo of the three of them.

> JODIE
>
> Right.
> This photo goes behind the bar.

She points to the kilts.

> JODIE
>
> And I'll need those back.

All three sit and finish their drinks.

> PETE
>
> Well, nice to meet you miss, hope to see you again soon.

Pete stands, hands his kilt too Jodie and turns to Mick.

> PETE
>
> I'm gonna go get the car, see you out front.

> MICK
>
> Ok mate, see you in a minute.

Mick stands, looks at Jodie

> MICK
>
> If you have finished here for the night, can I walk you home?

Jodie laughs and stands.

> JODIE
>
> Look, Mick. There's a million guys who come through

here every day.

Mick extends his arm.

JODIE

But not many gentlemen I suppose. (giggling)
How gallant, that would be nice.

3 The two walk down the steps to the river walk and turn right, Mick puts his arm around Jodie's waist as they walk and Jodie stops.

MICK

I'm sorry, I didn't mean to...

JODIE

No, we're here. This is my door.

Mick looks and sees they have stopped less then 200 yards down the walk from Mad Dog's, and they are standing outside a lobby door.

MICK

Blimey that was quick. I hoped I'd be with you a bit longer.

He looks at Jodie and holds her by the waist.

MICK

I'll be back in a couple of weeks. Be nice to see you then.

Jodie holds up Mick's left hand and looks for a ring.

JODIE

No wife?

                                MICK

No.
And no girlfriend.

Mick slowly pulls her close. They pause then kiss quickly on the
lips, they pull away, look at each other, then kiss again, longer,
both slowly wrapping their arms around each other.

                                MICK

I do like San Antonio!

Mick takes a pen from his pocket and writes several telephone
numbers on a piece of paper.

                                MICK

I'm six hours ahead of you, can you call me the day
after tomorrow?

                                JODIE

I will.

They separate. Jodie gives Mick a kiss on the cheek.

                                JODIE

Safe trip. One if by land, two if by sea, right?

                                MICK

What?

                                JODIE

(laughing) I'll call you!

Jodie smiles, turns, and walks into the apartment.

CUT TO:

INT. PETE'S CAR - SAN ANTONIO -EVENING

Mick gets into Pete's car, closes the door and they drive off.

PETE

Are you OK there pal?
You look a bit flush.

MICK

I'm fine mate.

Mick smiles and looks out the window.

MICK

Got to say son, you look good in a proper kilt.

PETE

You tell any one and the Met is gonna be short a
Sergeant.

CUT TO:

INT. HEATHROW AIRPORT,LONDON - AFTERNOON, ONE WEEK LATER

Pete and customs undercover agent NICK WESTON arrive at Heathrow International Airport, London. Pete introduces Nick to Mick, Robin to Pete and Nick.

MICK

There you are. You blokes have a good trip?

PETE

Hey man! I'm still drying out from San Antonio. Mick, this is Nick. Mick's our case agent here.

NICK

How do you do.

MICK

Pleasure. This is Robin Erwin, our technical officer.

ROBIN

Cheers. Nick, you don't sound like a Texan. Where did you get your English accent?

NICK

English class.

ROBIN

Wha....?

MICK

There has been a meeting change with the fat man tomorrow. Like I told you, we were supposed to meet but he called us up to tonight asking to move it.

ROBIN

That's impossible. You sound like you're from...

MICK

Robin, not now.

NICK

Oh bloody hell, we're getting off to a great start here aren't we.

PETE

Hey, what can you do.

MICK

It's just an introduction. He said he's bringing his shipper with him. We don't expect much more than them getting to know you.

NICK

I hope I didn't travel all this way just to say hello. What the hell. I've been up twenty hours already. I'll have this case made by the time I go to bed.

Everyone turns to leave. Pete looks at Mick, raises his eyebrows and winks. Mick shakes his head and smiles.

CUT TO:

INT. SURVEILLANCE VAN OUTSIDE INN ON THE PARK - EVENING
Mick, Robin and Pete are sitting in the rear of the technical surveillance van, waiting for the arrival of Omar Cor and the shipper at the restaurant.

ROBIN

Of course all communication is done in voice privacy. We use an encryption program....

MICK

Robin! They have bloody tech vans over there too! I'm
sure he's seen it all before!

PETE

Yeah, but we wouldn't have much of a case without you
would we?

Robin smiles.

MICK

Don't encourage him.
Right, now, here we go.

CUT TO:

INT. TOP FLOOR, INN ON THE PARK, HYDE PARK, LONDON - EVENING
*Omar and his partner DRAGON, walk up to the table. Dragon
is medium build with short military style hair and dark eyes. He
is quiet but speaks with a faint eastern European accent.
Steve and Nick stand up. They make introductions and sit down.*

OMAR

Steven, I have to apologise for the last minute change.
Dragon here's layover was shorter than we had expected.

*The waiter arrives and takes drink orders from Omar and Dragon.
Steve motions to the waiter.*

STEVE

On my bill please.

The waiter leaves.

CUT TO:

INT. SURVEILLANCE VAN - EVENING
Mick looks over to Pete.

MICK

Did he say Dragon?

Pete shrugs.
Mick makes a call to New Scotland Yard.

MICK

Intelligence office. Yes, the name is Dragon, white male, six foot two, stocky build. Get me anything you got.

CUT TO:

INT. INN ON THE PARK RESTAURANT, LONDON - EVENING

STEVE

Oh that's quite all right.

OMAR

My colleague here is in shipping and will coordinate loading your container. In addition, he can facilitate transportation to your final destination.

STEVE

That's great. I would prefer it though if he dealt with Nick directly from here on, on the U.S. end.

OMAR

You won't be coming over to the states?

STEVE

A situation is preventing me from traveling as freely as
I would like right now. A short term problem I'm sure.
More importantly to you though, Nick here will be
handling the financial details also.

OMAR

Nick, you look tired.

NICK

No rest for the wicked I suppose.

Everyone chuckles.

STEVE

Before we continue, we'll need a final quote.

*Everyone stops talking as the waiter returns with drinks and
leaves.*

OMAR

Yes, yes. I know I told you 'one' several weeks
back. I was having trouble ordering the plastic and
accompanying electronic items. I located those parts in
Nicaragua and can have the two shipments consolidated
for you in Africa.

CUT TO:

INT. SURVEILLANCE VAN - EVENING

PETE
Parts. He sounds like a fucking used car dealer.

CUT TO:

INT. TOP FLOOR, INN ON THE PARK, HYDE PARK, LONDON - EVENING

OMAR
Due to the consolidation logistics and bidding through
a secondary vendor
in Central America, my final quote is 'one point two'.

STEVE
One point two.

Steve looks at Nick.

CUT TO:

INT. SURVEILLANCE VAN - EVENING

PETE
C'mon boys, do your thing.

CUT TO:

INT. TOP FLOOR, INN ON THE PARK, HYDE PARK, LONDON - EVENING

NICK

The market price of the items on the list runs less than two hundred fifty thousand, plus what, two percent of that for shipping? That's quite a mark up you're asking us to shoulder.

OMAR

You're forgetting government licensing, shipping and manifest documentation.

Steve and Nick stare across the table, trying to control their anger.

DRAGON

Look, we bear the burden of furnishing proper documentation to the authorities for approval, both overseas and here. Those approvals don't come cheaply you know.

NICK

I understand. And what about insurance?

DRAGON

Insurance? What would you like? Lloyds of London?

Steve leans over the table, places his large hand on top of the Dragon's, staring at him ominously. Steve speaks in a low voice.

STEVE

What we expect is an assurance that the gear winds up

in our hands and not the Coast Guard's.

OMAR

Steven, please keep in mind, we're just brokers here.

STEVE

I do understand.

Steve releases the shippers hand and sits back.

STEVE

But bear in mind, my clients, your customers, don't share our sense of understanding.

A long pause in the conversation. Everyone is looking at each other digesting the last statement.

OMAR

Fine. If we were to agree on 'one' I normally require fifty percent in advance.

STEVE

I know 'one' was an estimate. If we could stay with that, I don't think my clients would object to raising your advance to eight hundred.

Omar man looks up at the ceiling for a minute.

OMAR

Done. One it is. It cuts into our mark up but I'm sure this will not be our last venture.

CUT TO:

INT. SURVEILLANCE VAN - EVENING

The phone rings.
Mick answers the phone, listens and hangs up.

> MICK
>
> Dragon owns a dry cleaners in North London.

> MICK
>
> He's involved in numerous missing persons inquiries and can move anything anywhere. There aren't any witnesses, all too scared of him. We don't have a current photo.

> PETE
>
> Babe, we got us a deal.

> MICK
>
> A tasty twosome son.

CUT TO:

INT. TOP FLOOR, INN ON THE PARK, HYDE PARK, LONDON - EVENING

> OMAR
>
> Very well then. Agreed?

Everyone shakes hands. They raise their drinks.

> OMAR
>
> And how do you wish to arrange the financing?

Steve looks at Nick.

NICK

Well with the bank reporting requirements being what they are these days, we would prefer to deal in cash. Eight hundred thousand delivered to, Dragon? Is it? At the docks in the states when we confirm the load is on board, the balance can be delivered as cash or wire transferred. Whichever you prefer. Problem?

DRAGON

Yes. I need a car with a bigger trunk!

Everyone laughs.

NICK

I can deliver a letter of credit to you if that's all right. Quite frankly, we're sitting on the funding right now. What port will we be shipping from?

DRAGON

Houston.

OMAR

And the destination?

STEVE

Liverpool.

DRAGON

Not a problem.

Omar stands up.

> OMAR
>
> Gentlemen, it has been a pleasure meeting you. Dragon, you can exchange contact numbers with Nick if you would. Expect a call from me in say, four weeks, just to keep you abreast of things. Can I give anyone a ride?

Everyone stands up. Dragon and Nick exchange numbers and business cards. They shake hands.

CUT TO:

INT. OMAR'S AUSTIN OFFICE - DAY
Omar is sitting at his desk, looks up startled to see Nick standing in the doorway. He pauses for a second to compose himself before acting happy to see him.

> OMAR
>
> Nick! I wish you had called. It's great to see you.

> NICK
>
> Yes, yes, good news all around. I think you'll enjoy seeing this.

Nick sits down and places a piece of paper in front of Omar.

> OMAR
>
> Ah, the letter of credit. Outstanding.

> NICK
>
> The bank and account numbers are on the bottom.

OMAR

Do you mind?

NICK

Not at all.

Omar picks up the telephone and calls the number on the paper.

OMAR

Everything's automated nowadays.

Omar looks at the paper, enters account numbers. He listens then hangs up the phone.

OMAR

Indeed it's all there. Outstanding Nick. Tell me. What is your schedule like this evening?

NICK

What did you have in mind?

OMAR

I thought you might want to take a preliminary look at what we have so far. Is nine o'clock all right?

NICK

I believe I can make that.

OMAR

Very well then. See you here tonight.

Nick leaves the office.

Omar picks up the phone and makes another call.

OMAR

Meet me in thirty minutes.

He hangs up the phone.

CUT TO:

CAR WASH WAITING ROOM - DAY
Omar and Dragon are standing next to each other in a car wash, standing at the glass partition, watching cars go through the automated wash line.

DRAGON

I guess they are for real then.

OMAR

Apparently.

DRAGON

And the paperwork?

OMAR

I'll start something shortly. I'm still waiting on a few items.

DRAGON

My guy at the port in Houston is retiring soon. I don't know how much longer he'll be there. I'm worried about shipping it after he's gone.

OMAR

And why is that cause for concern?

DRAGON

Concern? The obvious consequences for me if it got
seized down there.

OMAR

The load isn't going to be seized because it isn't going to
be shipped.

He pauses and looks at Dragon.

OMAR

I want you to take care of that.

DRAGON

Well that's a relief.

OMAR

My car is ready. Talk to you soon.

CUT TO:

INT. OMAR'S AUSTIN OFFICE - NIGHT

*Omar walks Nick out into a large warehouse behind the office.
Turning on overhead lights, revealing several ocean going forty
foot containers. Their footsteps echo in the building. They walk to
the back of one of the containers. Omar holds the 'shopping list'
in his hand.*

                          OMAR

Here we are.

Omar opens the lock, pulls the door handle and swings the steel door open, exposing wooden crates.

                          OMAR

Let me see. We have the rifles, pistols, all of the ammunition. Oh, here's something I wanted to show you.

Omar pulls down a long heavy black case. He looks at the shopping list then opens the combination on the case.

                          NICK

The Barrett.

                          OMAR

Yes indeed. One of two. Nasty looking isn't it.

Nick takes the rifle out and examines it. He puts it back in the case, takes out and looks through the scope.

                          NICK

I know it makes Kevlar a moot point now doesn't it? Our people will definitely be happy. And what of the rest?

                                                        CUT TO:

INT. PETE'S G-RIDE - NIGHT
Pete and a second agent are sitting in a car, lights out, a block away in a dimly lit parking lot full of cars. They are listening to

the conversation over a monitor. Pete gets on the radio:

> PETE
>
> Sounds like most of the stuff is there. The U/C is looking at the Barretts. Any movement outside over there?

> DONNA
>
> (through the radio) No, it's quiet.

> PETE
>
> Clear.

CUT TO:

INT. OMAR'S WAREHOUSE - NIGHT

> OMAR
>
> Everything is here with the exception of the plastic. We will be consolidating the shipments in Liberia before it is shipped to Liverpool.

> NICK
>
> Fantastic. When do you think you can have it shipped?

> OMAR
>
> As soon as we get word the plastic is on the way, we can forward this container. I don't think it would take too long.

Nick inspects the container.

NICK

Can I get a copy of the container number? They would like to have something on the other end.

OMAR

I don't see why not.

Omar writes numbers on a piece of paper and hands it to Nick. He closes and locks the doors to the container and turns to Nick.

OMAR

Dragon will contact you when he has a definite date and time.

NICK

Our clients are anxious to get this thing moving. What kind of time frame are we looking at?

OMAR

Again, it shouldn't take more than a week or two. He'll let you know.

CUT TO:

INT. PETE'S G-RIDE - NIGHT
Pete picks up the radio mike.

PETE

OK it sounds like we're done here.
Call him out when they leave. I'll see you guys tomorrow.

DISSOLVE TO:

INT. PETE' CUBICLE - DAY
Three weeks later, Pete is in his office, agitated, talking to Mick on the telephone.

> PETE
>
> I can't tell you what the problem is or if there's a problem at all.

> PETE
>
> We haven't heard from him since we met at the warehouse. He's checked the account twice since then but he's not returning Nick's calls. My boss is breaking my balls, the prosecutors are asking questions, the Attaché's starting to insinuate we fucked something up and ATF wants to wash their hands of it. The boss wants to give it another week before we shut it down. Has Steve heard from him?

CUT TO:

INT. MICK IN LONDON ON THE TELEPHONE AT WORK. - EVENING

> MICK
>
> No, it's the same here. My governors want to know what the problem is. I'm having to convince them this wasn't about scamming trips. Nick saw the load right?

> PETE'S VOICE
>
> (through the phone)

Yeah he saw the fucking load! We've been sitting on the warehouse since then and it's still in there. I knew this was going to go to shit.

MICK

What are you talking about? How many deals have you seen go off on time? Look, there's nothing more we can do but give it a little more time. We've done everything we can do.

CUT TO:

INT. PETE' CUBICLE - DAY

PETE

Yeah, right.
Tell that to my bosses.

MICK'S VOICE

(through the phone)
How about Thursday?

PETE

Do what?

CUT TO:

INT. MICK'S OFFICE - EVENING
Mick looks at airline tickets.

                              MICK

I'll be out there Thursday. a date in San Antonio.

                          PETE'S VOICE

I have
You gotta be kidding me. What, one
trip to the Alamo wasn't enough?

                              MICK

Very funny mate.

                                                    CUT TO:

INT. PETE' CUBICLE - DAY

                              PETE

Well I guess I'll see you Thursday. You can help me with
my resume.

                                                    CUT TO:

EXT. GAS STATION - DAY
*Two days later, Pete is at the pump, gassing up his car when his
cell phone rings.*

                              PETE

Hello.

                     LEONARD FILLMORE'S VOICE

(through the phone) Pete, it's Leonard over at
Commerce.

PETE

Hey, how you doing.

LEONARD FILLMORE'S VOICE

(through the phone) I think I have some news for you.
I got an application for a Shippers Export Declaration
from Liberia Consolidated Freight to export computers
to Africa.

Pete finishes gassing up. He looks out into the distance.

PETE

That's great. I'm sure internet dating's getting to be
popular over there.

LEONARD FILLMORE'S VOICE

(through the phone) No, no, no. Liberia Consolidated
Freight. I did some checking. Guess who owns it?

PETE

I'm listening.

LEONARD FILLMORE'S VOICE

(through the phone) Dragon is the president. Omar
Cor is the registered agent.

Pete takes the receipt from the pump.

PETE

You think this is it?

LEONARD FILLMORE'S VOICE

(through the phone) The application is for a forty foot container currently located at Tranquility Shipping here in town, said to contain sixteen hundred desk top computers. Total weight twenty seven thousand pounds. Scheduled to depart through the port of Houston via the motor vessel Ocean Trader on the thirtieth of the month.

PETE

Holy shit. Leonard, I gotta go. You're a prince man, I'll talk to you soon. Thanks.

CUT TO:

INT. JODIE'S APARTMENT - DAY

Mick is at Jodie's apartment stepping out of the shower when the phone rings. Jodie, wearing only an Arsenal football jersey, answers the phone and hands it to Mick.

MICK

Yeah? Are you sure? Really sure? Oh bollocks, right. See you soon.

Mick hands the phone back to Jodie who wonders about the conversation.

MICK

Love, the job's come off early. I've to go but I'll be back after.

JODIE

Take a key.

CUT TO:

INT. NICK'S OFFICE - AFTERNOON

Nick is at his Houston office working when an agent stops at his office door.

AGENT

Nick, you have a call on the UC line, number five.

NICK

Thanks, I'll get it. Nick gets up and walks to the far end of the office. He opens a heavy door and enters a small windowless room covered with papers and notes tacked to the wall. Below is a long table with a row of nine numbered telephones connected to tape recorders. Empty coffee cups, note pads and pens litter the table. Nick walks over to phone number five, with a red blinking light, hits the record switch to the recorder underneath, picks up the phone

NICK

Hello?

DRAGON

Nick this is Dragon.
How are you today?

NICK

Quite well thanks. How are things going? Good news I hope.

DRAGON

We have everything in order. I'm happy to say we will be shipping out next Wednesday.

NICK

Wednesday, that's ahh....

DRAGON

The thirtieth.

NICK

Excellent. We were getting a little worried not hearing from you.

DRAGON

Like I said, licenses and all.

DRAGON

I knew it would happen. Say, your container looks like it will be one of the last to go on board. Can you meet us at City Dock 19? We can have a look and take delivery of the advance.

NICK

Absolutely. Steve will be quite pleased. I imagine he'll want to be there.

                    DRAGON
I thought he had travel issues?

                     NICK
Yes, he says it's been sorted out.

                    DRAGON
That's great then. I'll call you during the day with a
time. Shipping schedules are about as accurate as the
airlines these days. We'll see you on the thirtieth.

                     NICK
Thanks, bye.

*Nick hangs up the phone, stops the recorder. He takes out the tape.
He turns around to an office phone sitting on a small table. Picks
it up and dials.*

                     NICK
Pete, it's Nick in Houston. Looks like we're on for the
thirtieth. Yeah, that's right. Start calling the troops and
we'll see you here Tuesday. I'm getting knighted after all
of this right? Ha ha, yeah right. Sure, I'll call Steve. See
you Tuesday.

Nick hangs up the phone.

                                              CUT TO:

INT. SPECIAL AGENT IN CHARGE HOUSTON CONFERENCE ROOM - DAY
*The long room is wrapped with tall glass windows. Several dozen
men and women, in office and casual attire, some with holstered*

guns and badges on their belts, are sitting and standing around a long table. Drinking coffee and bottled water. Everyone is talking and joking. The atmosphere is excited.

At the end of the room is a wall high eraser board with a hand drawn diagram of the Houston ship channel. Conspicuously written on the board are the headings: BUST SIGNAL, TAKE DOWN ASSIGNMENTS, PRIMARY/SECONDARY RADIO CHANNELS. Nick and diminutive looking Tech Agent MEADE, wearing glasses, sit silently under the diagram. Agent PAUL RAMOS, well built, short and serious looking, stands at the board, looks at his watch. Double doors to the room open. Pete, Mick, Steve and Robin enter and walk over to Nick. They make introductions, shakes hands then turn to the crowd.

PAUL RAMOS

All right folks, let's get started. Nick, you care to tee off first.

Nick turns to the crowd. Looking around the room.

NICK

Thanks Paul. Good morning class, everyone is here? The Austin crew is here? Good. With your help, and support from the tactical team here, We will be taking down a container full of weapons tomorrow down in the port. Just prior to this, the crooks are expecting delivery of eight hundred thousand dollars in cash that Pete here borrowed from Uncle Sam. Anyway, here's the Ops plan.

Nick starts handing out a stack of the operation plan.

DISSOLVE TO:

INT. SAC HOUSTON HALLWAY - DAY

Everyone is walking out of the conference room, some loitering in the hallway. Paul Ramos walks up to Pete and Mick.

PAUL RAMOS

Well we have at least twenty four hours. We'll see ya'll here tomorrow afternoon?

PETE

Sure thing. All we got left is to hurry up and wait.

Mick and Pete look back and see Dan and Robin holding a metal electrical box, intensely examining it. Both talking to each other at the same time.

MICK

Ah look. Kindred spirits, or should I say soul mates?

PETE

Speaking of which.

MICK

Shit, I need to call her.

Mick opens his cell phone and dials a number.

PETE

You haven't put her on speed dial yet? Some pro you are.

CUT TO:

INT. SPECIAL AGENT IN CHARGE HOUSTON CONFERENCE ROOM - *AFTERNOON - THE NEXT DAY*

Pete, Mick, Nick, Steve are sitting together at the long table quietly. A large military style duffel bag with the money sits on the table in front of them. No one is talking. The office phone on the table rings. Pete puts it on speaker.

PETE

Hello?

KEVIN

Hey it's Kevin. Omar left his office and we followed him to the airport. You're not gonna believe this, he just got on a private aircraft.

Pete, Mick, Nick and Steve look at each other concerned.

KEVIN

He's taxiing out right now.

PETE

Is it a charter flight? Where's he going?

KEVIN

No, he's flying it! Donna just called FAA. They said he filed a flight plan for Mexico City.

PETE

Mexico City! What the fuck!

Nick's cell phone rings. He looks at the number, turns and nods to

Steve, stands up and walks out of the room.

> PETE
>
> Thanks man. If there's any changes let us know.

> KEVIN
>
> You guys still going ahead with it?

> PETE
>
> I don't know now. We'll see.

Nick walks back into the conference room, cell phone in hand.

> NICK
>
> That was our boy. He wants to meet at seven thirty.

> MICK
>
> Decision time gentlemen. What do you want to do?

CUT TO:

INT. PRIVATE AIRCRAFT FLOWN BY FAT MAN - AFTERNOON
Omar is in flight, talking to Dragon on his cell phone.

> OMAR
>
> What I want you to do is call me when it's over and you have everything under control. I'll be on the ground by then. OK?

> DRAGON
>
> No problem. We'll make it quick.

Omar hangs up the cell phone.

CUT TO:

INT. SPECIAL AGENT IN CHARGE HOUSTON CONFERENCE ROOM - AFTERNOON

> PETE
> Look, everybody is in place but it's still your call.

> NICK
> Well, our business is with Dragon.

> STEVE
> We really don't need the target there.

> NICK
> The fat bastard would just drop dead from a heart attack during the take down anyway.

Steve and Nick laugh.

> PETE
> So you guys are OK with it?

> NICK AND STEVE
> Let's go.

CUT TO:

EXT. SURVEILLANCE VAN IN THE PORT - EVENING
Robin steps out of the van and walks out of ear shot.

Takes out his cell phone and calls Mick.

> ROBIN
>
> Mick. I don't know. If you ask me, we could use a few more cameras, and I think the audio reception could be better.

CUT TO:

INT. PETE'S G-RIDE - EVENING
Pete and Mick are driving down the highway to the port. Mick is talking to Robin on his cell phone.

> MICK
>
> Don't worry about them. Let them sort it out. Just stay out of their way unless they ask you to do something. Understand?

Mick hangs up the phone.

> MICK
>
> Already they're at it like a couple of old ladies down there.

CUT TO:

EXT. PORT OF HOUSTON MAIN ENTRANCE - EVENING
Tactical team agents sit in an unmarked car in traffic, follow Nick and Steve in a car as they approach the port gate. Tactical agents continue down the street as the U/Cs slowly turn into the port.

TACTICAL AGENT

All units, U/Cs just entered the main gate and heading your way.

CUT TO:

INT. SURVEILLANCE VAN - EVENING

DAN MEADE, another agent and Robin, inside the surveillance van parked at the top level parking lot over the docks. A few minutes later, they watch the monitor as the under-covers arrive several hundred yards away at city dock 19. Nick and Steve can be heard over the speakers. There are numerous tractor trailer trucks driving up and down the length of the docks.

MEADE

Clear. We have our guys on camera at the north west corner of the dock nineteen warehouse. We're getting good audio signal. The vessel is there.

CUT TO:

INT. TACTICAL AGENT VEHICLE - EVENING

An agent is in a car parked across the busy street from the main port entrance. He observes a tractor trailer carrying a forty-foot container slowly approach the gate. Taking a second look with binoculars, he sees the container numbers match the numbers shown on the ops plan. A car with three men are following right behind the container.

TACTICAL AGENT

All units, the package is at the gate followed by the target. The car is occupied three times.

CUT TO:

FULL SHOT U/C CAR WITH NICK AND STEVE PARKED OUTSIDE WAREHOUSE - EVENING

With truck traffic continuing to go by, the container slowly drives past Nick and Steve who are standing outside their car. The back of the truck stops right next to the trunk of the U/C car. Dragon and two men slowly pull up along the other side of the U/C car. All three men get out and shake hands.

CUT TO:

INT. SURVEILLANCE VAN - EVENING

Meade is watching the monitor, talking on the radio.

MEADE

OK, everyone's here meeting at the back of the truck. Standby. Wait a minute. The truck's pulling away, I've lost sight of the truck. Everyone is getting back in their cars and moving. Hold on, hold on. I've lost sight of the bad guys. Now they've stopped again. All I can see is the trunk of our car. Copy?

CUT TO:

INT. PETE AND MICK IN PETE'S G-RIDE PARKED SEVERAL HUNDRED
YARDS AWAY - EVENING

*Pete and Mick are sitting several warehouses away. Pete talking
into the mike.*

> PETE
>
> Clear. They're probably getting out of the traffic. Do
> you still have audio?

INT. SURVEILLANCE VAN - EVENING

Dan talks into the mike.

> MEADE
>
> Ten four, the trunk is up on our car. I can hear them
> opening the back of the container talking about the
> load. No visual of anyone and it's getting dark.

CUT TO:

INT. PETE AND MICK IN PETE'S G-RIDE PARKED SEVERAL HUNDRED
YARDS AWAY - EVENING

*Pete and Mick are listening to Dan's transmission. Tactical Agent
Paul Ramos comes on the air.*

> PAUL RAMOS
>
> If they've lost sight we need to move in.

> PETE
>
> No, standby, we'll go get a closer look. Fuck! We need
> to stay on that money.

Suddenly Mick starts to open his door.

> MICK
> I'll go down there.
> Do you have a radio I can use?

Pete pauses for a minute, then reaches into the back seat, picks up a hand held radio, turns it on, sets it to the proper channel, hands it to Mick. Mick gets out and starts to close the car door then pauses.

> MICK
> Say, you wouldn't have an extra one of those?

Mick nods at Pete's holster.

> PETE
> Wait a minute.

Pete reaches under his seat and pulls up a snub nose .357 revolver out of a holster. He hands the butt of the gun to Mick.

> PETE
> No cowboy shit down there OK?

Mick smiles and tucks the gun under his shirt.

> MICK
> I'll call you in a minute.

CUT TO:

INT. SURVEILLANCE VAN - EVENING
Dan, Robin and Agent are watching the monitor.
Dan is talking on the mike.

MEADE

Damn, it's getting dark down there. They're still talking down there but the audio is breaking up. There's less traffic down there now but we're having a hard time seeing anything, copy?

CUT TO:

EXT. MICK JOGGING QUIETLY ALONG WAREHOUSES - NIGHT
In the darkness, Mick is walking and jogging quietly along the warehouses around pallets of freight. It is still hot out, very humid, and he is sweating. He comes to the corner of the warehouse adjacent to warehouse nineteen twenty yards away. An occasional container truck with headlights on passes, throwing up dust and dirt. He can see all the players standing next to the truck and cars. He brings the radio to his mouth and whispers.

MICK

OK. Everyone is still standing at the vehicles. The trunk is still up on our car. Hold on. Everybody's walking into the warehouse now. (agitated) They keep changing the bloody script! I'm going to move around for a better look.

PETE'S VOICE

(through the radio)
Has the money moved?

MICK

No.

96

I don't believe so.

CUT TO:

INT. TACTICAL VAN - EVENING
Team leader PAUL RAMOS, sitting on a bench with eight other agents in full tactical gear, is irritated, gets on the radio.

> PAUL RAMOS
> Look, if we've lost the eye I'm going to give the order to move in!

CUT TO:

INT. PETE ALONE IN HIS G RIDE - EVENING

> PETE
> Just hold on. All the players are still in place and we have an eyeball on the ground. Standby a minute. Break. Dan, you hearing anything?

> DAN'S VOICE
> (through the radio)
> They're still coming in broken, but it sounds like they're still there.

CUT TO:

EXT. MICK ON THE GROUND - EVENING
Mick walks quietly to the opposite corner of warehouse nineteen, looking around for a window.

He finds a door with a window facing into the warehouse and peers in. In the dark, he looks through the dimly lit warehouse and open garage doors on the opposite side, to see two figures close the trunk to the U/C car, get in and drive off.

CUT TO:

INT. SURVEILLANCE VAN - EVENING
Meade, Robin and an agent's faces are lit up by the glow from the monitor. They are scanning both ends of the warehouse. They see an occasional tractor rig with a container drive past.

> MEADE
> Is that our U/Cs driving off?

CUT TO:

INT. PETE ALONE IN HIS G RIDE - EVENING
Pete holds the mike to his mouth.

> PETE
> Mick, are they gone?

CUT TO:

EXT. MICK LOOKING THROUGH DOOR WINDOW - NIGHT
Mick looks around and sees a window, walks over and looks in.

> MICK
> Our boys are gone but the crooks are sitting in their car. Can you give Nick a call?

PETE'S VOICE

(through the radio)
Clear. Everybody standby till I talk to the U/Cs. He's
not answering. Let me try again. Mick, can you get a
better look?

PAUL RAMOS' VOICE

(through the radio)
We need to secure that truck!

PETE

Just hold on for Christ sake!

CUT TO:

EXT. WAREHOUSE NINETEEN - NIGHT

*Mick slowly stalks around the warehouse to the corner closest to
the deal and peeks around the corner. Just ten feet from the crooks
car, pistol in hand, he can hear a cell phone ringing in the car. He
notices the truck and container are also gone. Pistol raised to his
side, staying in the shadows of the warehouse, he slowly side steps
until he stands along side the occupied car. He looks into the car,
cell phone still ringing, then suddenly jumps back, making a loud
bang against the corrugated metal warehouse wall with his back.
He screams into the radio.*

MICK

Get down here now! Hurry!
Get everyone down here!

CUT TO:

INT. PETE ALONE IN HIS G RIDE - NIGHT

Pete curses to himself and picks up the mike.

PETE

Tac team copy? Move in!

CUT TO:

EXT. WAREHOUSE NINETEEN - NIGHT

Mick is sweeping the area with the pistol in hand, breathing and sweating heavily. Car engines racing in the darkness from all directions are getting closer, then screeching to a stop. A spotlight turns on Mick, blinding him.

TACTICAL AGENT

Throw the gun away from you and lay on the ground. Do it now.

Tires are screeching in the darkness, a car door slams and footsteps are heard running out of the darkness up to Mick.

PETE

He's a good guy! Don't shoot! He's one of us! Mick just put it down!

Tactical agents run around Mick and Pete into the warehouse. Other agents surround the car, pointing MP5 machine guns and spot lights at it. Paul Ramos walks over and looks into the car, reaches in, then quickly steps back, looking at his hand.

PAUL RAMOS

Oh Jesus.

Saying nothing, Mick squats down putting his head in his hands.

CUT TO:

P.O.V. INTERIOR CROOKS CAR - NIGHT
Pete, confused, walks over to the car and looks in. He sees Nick in the drivers seat, staring ahead, slack jawed, dead. The handle of an ice pick protrudes just forward of his left ear. Steve is slumped to the side in the passenger seat. His throat is cut, a stream of blood draining from his mouth into a coagulated pool in his lap. Shocked and pale, pistol in hand, Pete turns and sits on the ground with his back leaning against the bottom of the open car door. He looks over at Mick who won't look up.

CUT TO:

ANGLE ON ICE PICK IN NICKS HEAD
Blood trickles down along the ice pick. Pete doesn't notice as it slowly drips blood onto his shoulder. Paul Ramos walks over and stands in front of Pete, looking down at him, MP5 slung on his side. He kicks Pete in the foot.

PAUL RAMOS

You're in my way.

DISSOLVE TO:

INT. DRAGON AND CROOK DRIVING THE UC CAR - NIGHT
Driving down the highway in the U/C car, Dragon in the passenger

seat, following the container truck. Dragon has a cell phone up to his ear. Passing street lights rhythmically light the inside of the car.

DRAGON

Hello? Yes. How was your flight? Almost there? That's good. Yes, of course. We're done here. We'll see you in a few days. Right. Bye.

Dragon and the driver look as several ambulances with lights and sirens speed past in the opposite direction towards the port. Dragon dials a number on his cell phone. He stares out into the highway while talking.

DRAGON

Hey hun. Thought I'd give you a call before we stopped to eat. Is my baby girl still up? Put her on. Hi sweetie, isn't it bedtime?

FADE OUT:

FADE IN:

INT. BUSH INTERCONTINENTAL AIRPORT - AFTERNOON - RAINING

Mick, Robin and Pete are standing next to each other, away from the large crowd at the departure gate, staring silently through the glass at a British Airways 747. Boarding announcements are heard in the background. All three are dirty and un-shaven.

PETE

Look. Mick. What are you looking at back there?

Mick stares at Pete in a daze. He speaks in a flat voice.

MICK

I'm meeting with my Governor, the Detective
Superintendent and probably the Commander in the
morning.

Mick runs his fingers through his greasy hair.

MICK

Robin and I have to give statements. They will be
sending investigators out here I'm sure.

PETE

No man. I mean you.

MICK

Me? I don't know. This has never happened before. I
don't know what's going to happen.

*The gate agent announces final boarding. All three shuffle toward
the line. Robin starts to breath heavy as if he doesn't want to board.
Mick turns to Pete.*

MICK

You'll let me know when you find them?

PETE

Yeah. Yeah, sure.
They're out there now looking.

*A little boy standing in front of the three pulls on his mothers
coat, pointing through the window, down at the open hold of the
aircraft.*

LITTLE BOY

Mommy. What's that?

First Mick, then Pete and Robin unconsciously look out to where the boy is pointing and see a crated coffin, marked; 'Human Remains. Handle With Dignity.' Stencilled on the top. It contains Steve, slowly rolling up the conveyor into the hold. Robin starts to sob.

ROBIN

Oh Christ....

Mick puts his arm around Robin, ushering him towards the jetway. Pete walks along side them.

MICK

I guess we'll be in touch.

PETE

Mick.

MICK

Yes.

PETE

We'll get 'em.

Mick shrugs his shoulders.

MICK

I know. Right?

CUT TO:

INT. FRONT DOOR TO TRANQUILITY SHIPPING - AFTERNOON

The waiting room of Tranquility Shipping is empty and silent. The lights are on. Blinds are drawn. There is no activity. The office is dead still. Suddenly, the front door violently implodes from an explosive shaped charge. Glass sprays everywhere, the door and frame fly across the room. One second later, a larger, deafening explosion is heard in the back warehouse. Framed wall prints fall, ceiling tiles start to fall, cascading on top of desks and furniture. Through a fog of debris, tactical agents slowly, almost casually, stepping over debris, walk into the office from the front and rear of the building, weapons pointed down.

Meeting in the waiting area, they walk through the receptionists area to a closed door. An agent tries the door and it is locked. He steps back and raises his leg to kick the door, when the TEAM LEADER puts his hand on his shoulder.

TEAM LEADER

Hold on a second. DJ, you got one left?

DJ

Yeah, hold on.

DJ walks up and pulls from a satchel bag, a saline solution intravenous bag, wrapped in detonation cord and duct tape, and hangs it on the door knob. Agents start to step back.

DJ

Clear!

DJ detonates the bag. Water vaporizes and the door blows off the

105

hinges. More ceiling tiles fall. The team leader turns on the light while he and an another agent walk into the office. Surveying an empty office, the team leader brings the hand held radio to his mouth.

TEAM LEADER

Let me call the boss. Bravo one twelve to one O one.

VOICE

(through the radio) One O one, go ahead.

TEAM LEADER

We're clear here. It's what we expected.

VOICE

(through the radio) Ten Four.

DISSOLVE TO:

INT/EXT. LOCATIONS - VARIOUS, - DAY/NIGHT
(MONTAGE)
Mick and Robin are hurried off the flight by four stone faced Metropolitan Police Officers, holding them by the arm, around photographers, to a waiting police car, in the rain. Pete is standing in the back at Nick's funeral. Agents point him out to the family. Pete looks down at the casket going into the ground.
Looking up from the casket is Mick at Steve's funeral. Steve's mother walks up and slaps Mick in the face.
Mick talks to Pete on a cell phone in a car in a cold rainy night. Mick says he's doing great, will talk soon. Hangs up, lies down,

pulls a blanket over him.

Pete is sitting at night in front of the TV. He hangs up the cell phone. An empty scotch bottle is in his hand and a pistol next to him on the couch. He looks down at the pistol.

An American judge reads a report stating no criminal intent was discovered.

A British panel says the investigation was racked by incompetence. Suspects whereabouts are unknown. Case closed.

An older Mick turning in retirement paperwork. Clerk says everything is in order, gives him an insincere best wishes.

An older Pete emptying out his desk in a dingy, one man office. Stops at the door and turns out the light.

(END OF MONTAGE)

FIFTEEN YEARS LATER

CUT TO:

INT. AUSTIN INTERNATIONAL AIRPORT ARRIVALS TERMINAL- AFTERNOON

Pete is standing in the lobby area, wearing jeans, open dress shirt and loafers. Sunglasses hanging off the front. His hair is long and thinned out and he has put weight on. Holding car keys in his hand. Looking up at the arrival board, then the passenger arrival gate. PA announcements in the background, people coming and going. A crowd from an arriving flight spills into the lobby, mingling with people waiting. He thinks he sees Mick then continues looking around. Mick stops and looks, then smiles and walks around the crowd, surprising Pete. Mick, with a carry on bag, is wearing slacks and a short sleeve shirt, graying hair, looking thirty pounds heavier. Reading glasses hang from the front of his shirt. They shake hands. They continue to shake while talking.

MICK

Some investigator you are son. I spotted you from the plane. Nice hair mate.

PETE

Hey at least I have some left.

PETE

And I'm a civilian now too, thank you very much. You look good, Mick.

Pete points to the glasses.

PETE

You also using those now?

MICK

About four years. Yes, I put a little weight on to. Spent some quality time with Mr. Jameson.

They start to walk to the luggage pick up sign.

PETE

Well I gotta tell ya, this road trip has been a long time coming.

MICK

How many times have you been to Las Vegas?

PETE

Oh, a couple. It's a good place to get lost and relax. I think you'll like the drive. It's awhole lotta nothing between here and there.

CUT TO:

EXT. AIRPORT PARKING LOT EXIT - AFTERNOON
Their car leaves a pay booth, following signs to Interstate

CUT TO:

INT. PETE'S CAR - AFTERNOON
Pete driving, Mick in the passenger seat.
Pete puts a CD in

the console.

                    PETE

I figure three or four days if we take our time. How do you feel about hitting some old haunts first?

Mick looks melancholy at Pete.

                    MICK

I guess.
I don't see why not.

                    PETE

We don't have to. I figured, stop for a drink to better times and be done with it. You know? It's on the way.

                    MICK

Have you been back there?

                    PETE

Naw. I couldn't get myself to go. I thought it'd be better if we both went. You know, if you want to.

                    MICK

Sure, why not.

                    PETE

Hey, I gotta ask.
Have you kept in touch with her?

MICK

I tried. I just didn't know how to separate her from everything else. It never seemed like a good time to call, you know? And with the time passing and all. She didn't miss anything. But to answer your question, I did reach out for her and tell her I was coming over.

PETE

Hey, we're not kids anymore and it's a little late to play hard to get. Give her a shout when we get there.

CUT TO:

EXT. BOTTOM STAIRS MAD DOG PUB SAN ANTONIO - EVENING
Pete and Mick stand at the bottom of the stairs looking up at the bar. Pete slaps Mick on the back as they start up the stairs.

PETE

C'mon, first ten are on me.

MICK

We're not staying long?

CUT TO:

INT. MAD DOG PUB - EVENING
Crowded and noisy, Mick and Pete are sitting at a table, drinks in hand, looking around. Pete holds up his glass.

PETE

Thanks for coming brother. You won't regret this.

Wasn't I right about calling her?

MICK

Cheers mate. She spoke to me. I'm going to see her in a few days. It hasn't got any quieter here has it. I wonder if they still serve.... Oh bollocks!

Mick jumps up pushing through the crowd towards the far wall. Pete gets up and follows. Pete finds Mick staring at a wall of pictures taken from within the bar. Pete suddenly realises what he is looking for.

PETE

Did you find it?

Mick scans the wall hoping to find the Polaroid of them taken years earlier. It is nowhere to be found.

MICK

No.
That was stupid to think so.

PETE

C'mon, let's go eat.

CUT TO:

INT. ITALIAN RESTAURANT ON THE SAN ANTONIO RIVERWALK - EVENING
Pete and Mick are seated at a table finishing dinner, drinking red wine. Mick excuses himself and leaves for the rest room. Pete, facing the front door, watches a small group of business men walk towards the door and stop to talk. Pete gazes around the other

tables, looks at his watch, bored.

CUT TO:

P.O.V. PETE SITTING AT THE TABLE - EVENING

Pete glances again to the party at the door. He sees a large, tall man in the party walk out the door. Pete turns pale, eyes squint, then open wide, he leans forward. The group at the door opens to reveal Omar in the party, shaking hands, smiling, then disappearing out the door with the group.

CUT TO:

INT. BEHIND PETE SITTING AT THE TABLE - EVENING

A hand rests on Pete's right shoulder. Pete, staring at the door, jumps back in his seat, dropping his drink on his pants and the floor.

PETE

Shit!

MICK

Whoa, easy there son!

A waitress runs over with a dinner napkin. She blots up the spill

WAITRESS

I'm sorry sir. Here, let me get that.

MICK

Well that's it for you. Some trip this is going to be.

Mick sits down and sees that Pete is distressed. Pete is trying to dry the spill on his pants.

113

MICK

Are you all right?

PETE

Yeah, yeah, sure. I don't know what happened.

MICK

Well for one you need to relax. Look at you. Still sitting facing the door. Watching the crowd. I bet you know what color shirt the bloke behind you is wearing.

PETE

Old habits I guess.

WAITRESS

Can I get you another drink?

PETE

Please. Can we get a round of Sambuca? Maybe I can hold on to that.

The waitress returns with drinks.
Mick and Pete down the shot and wipe their mouths.

PETE

I tell you what, let's get rooms here for the night. I used to have a hook at the Hilton. If she's still their maybe she can set us up. You up for that?

CUT TO:

INT. HILTON HOTEL RESTAURANT - ON THE RIVERWALK - MORNING

Mick and Pete are sitting at a table inside, on the second floor split level open air restaurant, facing the reception desk, lobby and glass elevators. Mick is in a jovial mood, making small talk about calling and meeting Jodie, eating breakfast. Pete is drinking coffee and looks like he hasn't slept at all. The outdoor patio overlooking the Riverwalk, lined with tables and umbrellas can be seen through the fifty foot high glass wall. Business people hurry through the lobby on their way to appointments. Tourists in t-shirts and shorts, walk through the revolving doors leading out to the patio and Riverwalk. Pete, scanning all of the activity in front of him, misses putting the coffee cup in the saucer, spilling it. His hand starts to shake. He stops and stares.

PETE

No! No! No way!

MICK

What the hell is the matter with you?

Pete, staring at the lobby, grabs a knife from the table and tries to stand up. Mick grabs his arm and holds him in his seat. He tries to keep his voice down.

MICK

Pete. What the bloody hell are you...!

Pete stares into the lobby.
Squeezing the knife, the blade cuts into his hand.

PETE

Look.

Mick looks over at the crowded lobby, squinting, scanning the crowd.

CUT TO:

P.O.V. HILTON HOTEL RECEPTION LOBBY - ON THE RIVERWALK - MORNING

In the crowded lobby, Omar is seen pacing in front of the reception desk, looking at his watch. He walks over to the glass elevator and takes it one flight down. He exits and walks over to the revolving doors. Looks around and returns to the lobby desk. Omar is met by two Hispanic males. They shake hands and disappear into the crowd, walking out towards the hotel entrance.

MICK

(angrily) You knew he was here.

Pete wraps his bleeding hand in a napkin.

PETE

If I had known, there'd be nothing but crime scene tape around that lobby.

MICK

You saw him last night didn't you! Why didn't you tell me!

PETE

Tell you what? That I'm fucking losing it? I still can't

believe it. This ain't happening.

MICK

No? Are you serious? That was him all right.

Mick looks at his watch and pulls a cell phone out of his pocket, dials a number.

MICK

Hello love. Yes of course we're still here. We got rooms over at the Hilton last night. Look. Pete's come up ill and I'm not sure what the problem is. I'm not sure about tonight but I'll call you this afternoon and let you know. Is that all right? Great. You're the best. Thanks love. Bye.

Mick turns to Pete.

MICK

Well, now what?

CUT TO:

INT. HILTON HOTEL BAR - NEXT TO THE LOBBY - EVENING
Mick and Pete are sitting on stools at a table in the dimly lit bar looking out into the lobby. Both are drinking club soda. Empty glasses fill the table.

MICK

Well I won't ask how much longer we're going to sit here.

PETE

No don't.

MICK

How do you know he's staying here?

PETE

I don't, but he was here first thing this morning and he
seems to know his way around the lobby pretty well.
Besides, where else would we start looking?

A waitress walks over to the table.

WAITRESS

You know fellas, we serve real drinks here too.

MICK

Thanks love, we're fine for now.

WAITRESS

I love that accent! Where are you from? Australia?

Pete looks out into the lobby.

PETE

Heads up Mick.

CUT TO:

P.O.V. HILTON HOTEL BAR - NEXT TO THE LOBBY - EVENING

*Omar and the two Hispanic males walk into the lobby and straight
into the bar, past Mick and Pete. They both freeze.*

MICK

Looks like you have customers hun.

Omar and the two Hispanics sit near the bar. The waitress brings back two beers. Omar stands up and shakes hands. He is overheard saying he'll see them tomorrow and walks out. Moments later the two men throw bills on the table, stand up and leave. Pete gets up and follows them.

CUT TO:

INT. ELEVATOR - HILTON - EVENING
Elevator door opens on the tenth floor. Both Hispanic men and a tourist couple walk out. Pete follows, carrying tourist brochures. Both men stop at room 1081 and go in. Pete walks by.

CUT TO:

INT. HILTON HOTEL BAR - NEXT TO THE LOBBY - EVENING
Pete goes back to the table Mick is sitting at.

PETE

1081

MICK

Right.

CUT TO:

P.O.V. HILTON HOTEL RECEPTION LOBBY - ON THE RIVERWALK - EVENING
Pete and Mick watch the lobby from their seats.
Pete looks back at the bar when Mick bumps his arm.

                              MICK

Hey, there they go.

Pete tosses cash on the table, he gets up to walk to the lobby.

                              PETE

I'll call you. Good luck upstairs.

                                                    CUT TO:

INT. RESERVATION DESK - HILTON HOTEL - EVENING
*Mick walks slowly up to the reception area, spotting a discarded
room card in an ashtray, he picks it up and walks
behind a drunk, belligerent tourist and his wife at the desk. Mick
looks over his shoulder and smiles at the clerk. A crowd of late
arrivals with luggage start to line up behind Mick.*

                        BELLIGERENT TOURIST

A king bed! That's what we asked for dammit! You gave
me twin beds and no, I'm not pushing them together!

                              CLERK

I'm terribly sorry sir. Let me see what the problem is.

                        BELLIGERENT TOURIST

Your reservationist has her head up her ass, that's the
problem!

*The clerk rushes over to another computer. Mick follows him and
pushes the room card across the counter.*

MICK

I'm sorry mate. I know you have your hands full, but
my room card isn't working. Do you have a second to
swipe me another one?

BELLIGERENT TOURIST VOICE

Drove half way across the damn state for this!

The clerk sighs without looking up.

CLERK

Room number?

MICK

1081.

The clerk swipes a card and hands it to Mick.

MICK

Thanks mate. Cheers.

CUT TO:

INT. ELEVATOR - HILTON - EVENING

*Mick walks out of the elevator on the tenth floor. He looks for a
room sign then follows it to 1081. He puts his ear to the door for a
second, looks both ways down the hallway then puts the card in the
lock. The lock clicks open and Mick walks in, closes the door, locks
the door and puts the chain on. Mick looks around and walks over
to the writing table, picking up a Samsonite briefcase sitting next
to it. He shuffles through the paperwork, examines two Mexican
passports and stops on a file, opening it. He looks at several forms*

in triplicate and tears off the back copies of each.
His cell phone rings.

MICK

Yes.

PETE'S VOICE

(through the phone) Hey I'm back. I lost them.

MICK

OK. I'm almost done.

Mick continues looking through the briefcase. He suddenly hears a room card being inserted into the door. He freezes, then hears the card being tried again. He hears muffled angry voices speaking Spanish on the other side of the door as they try the door handle. He picks up an empty beer bottle out of the trash can and quietly walks to the door. He hears the voices fade down the hallway.

CUT TO:

INT. TWO MEN WALKING TO TENTH FLOOR ELEVATOR - EVENING
Two irate men walk into the elevator looking at their door cards. Cursing in Spanish. The door closes.

CUT TO:

EXT. DOOR FOR ROOM 1081 - EVENING
The door opens. Mick walks out casually, quietly closes the door, then walks to the fire stairway door and leaves.

CUT TO:

INT. PETE AND MICK'S ROOM - HILTON - EVENING

Pete is sitting between the end of a twin bed and the desk as Mick walks in. They begin looking at the documents.

> PETE
>
> Shit, I guess we weren't hallucinating after all. It's a Bill of Lading for a shipment of after market mufflers.

Pete flips through the papers.

> PETE
>
> The manifest shows it scheduled for delivery tomorrow to a company called Auto Masters here in San Antonio. Our buddy's got a company called First Fleet Shipping.

> MICK
>
> Auto Masters.

Mick pulls out a phone book and searches it.

> MICK
>
> No.
> No listing.

> PETE
>
> 766 River Road in San Antonio.

> MICK
>
> Nope.

                              PETE

Hey, check this out. Pete hands Mick a business card.

                              MICK

First Fleet Shipping, 766 River Road, San Antonio
Texas. In the muffler business now is he? What do you
think it is? Dope?

                              PETE

I don't know.

Pete picks up the room phone.

                              PETE

But we're gonna find out.

                                                    CUT TO:

INT. CUSTOMS COMMUNICATION CENTRE WASHINGTON D.C. - NIGHT

*Rows of open, manned telephone consoles line a huge dimly lit
room. There is a din of noise, talking, computer printers, phones
ringing, radio traffic. Electronic maps, world clocks and computer
screens line the walls. A phone rings at a work station. A hand
reaches for the phone, pushing the line button. ART CONWAY
wearing a headset, answers.*

                           ART CONWAY

U.S. Customs Communications Center. Conway.

CUT TO:

INT. PETE AND MICK'S ROOM - HILTON - EVENING
Pete is sitting on the end of the bed talking on the phone. Mick is going over the papers.

> PETE
> Yes sir. I'd like to report a large load of contraband coming through the port of Laredo tomorrow morning.

CUT TO:

INT. CUSTOMS COMMUNICATION CENTER WASHINGTON D.C. - NIGHT

> ART CONWAY
> Contraband. Can you be a little more precise?

CUT TO:

INT. PETE AND MICK'S ROOM - HILTON - EVENING

> PETE
> No I can't. It's a forty-foot
> container consigned as after market mufflers going to San Antonio. You figure it out. I want you to give me a case number to this information when we're done so I know you followed through on it. You ready to copy?

CUT TO:

INT. CUSTOMS COMMUNICATION CENTRE WASHINGTON D.C. - NIGHT
Art Conway types on a computer keyboard.

ART CONWAY

Right. Right. Got it. I have a case number for you. It's going to be; T, Tom two seven zero eight Y Yankee C Charles. I'll pass this on to the Laredo duty agent now.

CUT TO:

INT. PETE AND MICK'S ROOM - HILTON - EVENING

Pete is sitting on the bed, on the phone, writing down the information.

PETE

Got it.

ART CONWAY'S VOICE

Should I bother to ask you for a name?

PETE

Sure. Serendipity.

ART CONWAY'S VOICE

Serendipity?

PETE

Yes Mr. Conway. I'll call you tomorrow.

Pete hangs up the phone.

MICK

Serendipity - you sure?

                         PETE

It's the best I could come up with. You heading out?

                         MICK

I guess we've done enough damage for one night.

Mick stands up and heads for the door.

                         MICK

I'll see you later.

                                              CUT TO:

INT. JODIE'S APARTMENT - NIGHT

*Mick knocks on Jodie's door. He stands nervously, looking at himself
in the windows reflection. The door opens. Jodie stands wearing
black leggings and a gray jumper with a belt around her. She smiles
and steps to the side.*

                         JODIE

    Come in.

                         MICK

    Thanks.

*Mick walks into the living room up to the T.V. and turns around.
As he turns, he sees the picture of himself and Pete taken at the
Mad Dog.*

                         MICK

    So, you took it.

JODIE

For old times sake. Would you like a drink?

MICK

Scotch please.

Jodie pours drinks while Mick looks around the apartment. Jodie hands Mick his drink and stands in front of him. She stares into his face.

JODIE

Was it bad?

MICK

Indescribable. I tried. God knows I tried to call you. I didn't know what to say. What to do, or where my head was.

JODIE

I wanted to call too. I didn't know if you needed me.

They both smile at each other.

MICK

It's so good to see you.vcYou haven't changed a bit.

JODIE

That's nice.

Mick leans forward and kisses Jodie on the lips. He pulls back. They kiss again. They put their glasses down and start pulling at each others clothes. Jodie walks backwards pulling Mick into the bedroom. Falling onto the bed, they take each other's clothes off, make love and drift asleep.

CUT TO:

EXT. FIRST FLEET SHIPPING - NIGHT
Pete is in his car, looking on the dashboard at a Garmin. He looks up as his headlights shine up on a street sign showing River Road.

> PETE
>
> Seven six six, seven six six.

He follows it to First Fleet Shipping, drives by and parks in the dark. Cars and trucks are parked out front. There are fork lifts moving crates in the warehouse. Omar walks out of the warehouse and walks up to an SUV. Two men get out of the SUV. Pete stares.

> PETE
>
> I'll be God damned.

Three men are standing by a car. One turns towards Pete's car, talking on a cell phone. It is Dragon.

CUT TO:

INT. JODIE'S APARTMENT - MORNING
Mick is getting dressed while Jodie lays on the bed in her Arsenal football shirt.

> MICK
>
> I'm glad you kept the shirt, darling.

Mick kisses Jodie on the head.

MICK

I've got to go meet Pete at the hotel. I'll see you back
here later.

JODIE

I don't suppose you still have the key?

*Mick reached into his pocket and holds up her apartment key on
a chain. Jodie smiles. Mick winks and leaves.*

CUT TO:

INT. HILTON HOTEL RESTAURANT - ON THE RIVERWALK - MORNING
*Mick and Pete are eating breakfast. Mick is shaking his head,
looking around, keeping his voice low.*

MICK

Are you positively sure?

PETE

I used to go to bed every night dreaming about
strippers. Since then, every night, those are the last two
faces on this planet I can see. That was him. Speaking of
which, how is your love life?

MICK

I've still got it mate.

Mick looks at his watch.

MICK

It's nine thirty. Don't you think you should call the

Customs Center? They should know something by now, right?

PETE

Yeah, I'll give it a little bit longer. OK here we go.

CUT TO:

P.O.V. HILTON HOTEL RESTAURANT - ON THE RIVERWALK - MORNING
The two Mexicans walk with Omar and Dragon through the lobby. One of the Mexicans has his arm locked around Dragon's, he keeps looking behind them. Omar is talking and very animated with his hands. They get on an empty glass lined elevator. Omar is still talking with his hands. The Mexicans aren't speaking. The elevator goes past the tenth floor to the top floor. All four get off.

CUT TO:

INT. HILTON HOTEL RESTAURANT - ON THE RIVERWALK - MORNING
Mick and Pete watch the elevator.

PETE

That's strange.

MICK

Do they have a room we don't know about?

CUT TO:

FULL SHOT - RIVER WALK TOUR BOAT - MORNING
A tour boat packed with tourists, meanders around a bend on

the river. The driver, who is also a guide, is giving a talk on the history of the river.

TOUR GUIDE

Right around the corner to your left is the beautiful, twelve story, three hundred room Hilton Palacio Del Rio, built in 1966. For those of you who want to walk to the Alamo, I'll be stopping there to let passengers off.

CUT TO:

FULL SHOT RIVER WALK TOUR BOAT - MORNING

All the passengers look forward as the boat comes around the corner to dock in front of the hotel. As they look up at the Hilton, their collective look changes from joy and admiration to absolute horror. They all scream together in unison. MOTHERS try to cover their CHILDREN'S faces.

CUT TO:

EXT. HILTON HOTEL - MORNING

Dragon, screaming, comes hurtling down the side of the hotel, the river and tourist barge is in the background. He hits an awning, loses an arm, continues through a patio umbrella and crashes loudly into a table. The table, chairs and glassware are destroyed by the impact.

CUT TO:

INT. HILTON HOTEL RESTAURANT - ON THE RIVERWALK - MORNING

Screams begin to build, echoing inside the lobby. There is a panic as people begin to run towards the river and out the the front of the hotel. People are running in all directions outside. Some are falling into the river. Mick and Pete sit quietly at their table watching. Mick looks back at the elevator.

MICK

They're coming back down. Looks like they're one short. Somebody had a bad night.

Pete clenches his teeth in a mock grimace.

PETE

Guess I'll make that phone call.

CUT TO:

INT. HILTON HOTEL RESTAURANT - ON THE RIVERWALK - MORNING
Pete gets up and walks away. Mick stands up and walks over towards Omar, pleading with the two Mexicans. In the midst of all the panic, he stops within earshot of their conversation.

OMAR

You can have it all. I promise you it's bigger than this shipment, more than enough for what you need. I swear! I'll bring it to my ranch out west. Give me two weeks. Just take it! Look, here's my number there. Five two zero, four three five.

*EMT's and firemen hurry through the lobby with stretchers. People are being ushered out of the lobby.
A police officer runs up to Mick and orders him to leave the lobby.*

CUT TO:

INT. HILTON HOTEL - PAY PHONE - MORNING

Pete is on a pay phone, his hand covering his ear to muffle all the shouting and commotion.

> PETE
>
> They did? That's great. What time did it happen? Great. How much did you say you'd pay? Wow. No, I don't want to talk to anybody. Maybe later. I'll be in touch.

Pete hangs up the phone.

CUT TO:

INT. PETE AND MICK'S ROOM - HILTON - MORNING

Mick is sitting on the end of the bed. Pete walks in, locks the door behind him.

> PETE
>
> Well, the vacation's paid for.

> MICK
>
> Are you ready for some more good news? No wait. What happened?

> PETE
>
> They hit the container at four this morning at the port of entry in Laredo. Behind six pallets of car mufflers, they found eight hundred kilos of Detagell. It's an industrial explosive. Comes in a kind of liquid slurry. The driver left the license for it in his other pants I guess.

MICK

My God. If that had hit the street.

PETE

Yeah. (sarcastically) No telling what they were going to
do with those mufflers. From what we saw this morning
they must figure they got a leak somewhere.

PETE

Too bad they didn't toss that fat little bastard off to. Did
you come up with anything?

MICK

Oh this is the dogs bollocks. You may get your wish yet.
He's got another load he said he'd turn over to them.
He's got a ranch of some sort out west where he'll bring
it in. I have part of a telephone number.

Mick looks at a piece of paper.

MICK

Five two zero area code. I looked it up. It's out in
Arizona. The exchange he gave is southern Arizona. I
called information and they had no listing for fat man
out there.

PETE

That sucks.

Mick holds up the shipping document.

MICK

Not really. Our friend they're scraping up downstairs is
listed out there.

PETE

No shit?

MICK

The No Le Hace Ranch. They gave a P.O. Box on
highway eighty. Any idea where it's at?

*Pete goes to his suitcase and pulls out a U.S. road map. He lays
it on the bed and slowly folds it open, one, two, three, four times.
Pete and Mick stare at the map. Pete points to the map.*

PETE

Right there.

MICK

Does that say Tombstone?

PETE

Well, what do you say?

MICK

Hey, call me Wyatt Earp.
I need to go see Jodie first.

CUT TO:

INT. PETE'S CAR - DAY
Pete and Mick enter the highway on ramp.
Overhead sign says 'Interstate 10 West'.

PETE

I bet she was real happy when she heard the news huh?

MICK

Man, if I survive this with her, she's a keeper.

PETE

You know. I got to thinking. It's gonna be tough trying to do anything out there by ourselves. We got lucky this one time.

MICK

Luck.
Is that what it was?

PETE

Yeah. Don't start. All my contacts end in El Paso and pick up in L.A.

MICK

Let me try somebody.
You're not too picky I hope.

Mick pulls out his cell phone and makes a call.

CUT TO:

INT. PIRATE RADIO STATION - DOVER ENGLAND - NIGHT

Archie Bell and the Drells; Do The Tighten Up, plays in the background of a darkened smoke filled room. Tattered old 60's rock an roll posters line the walls. Panels of foam egg-crate sound proofing are missing on the walls. An end table holding a lava lamp and a Siamese fighting fish in a small bowl, sits next to a rusty old microphone stand. A twenty-something year old girl in a pleated dress, lighting an alabaster marijuana pipe, sits crossed legged on a cot, staring off into space. A voice is heard talking over the music. A home made DJ booth built out of broken Plexiglas and bare 2X4's, containing a stack of electronics, reveals the back of a man sporting a long pony tail, slouching over a microphone. Two turn tables set in front of him next to a stack of LP records and an old push button business phone.

CUT TO:

INT. PIRATE RADIO STATION - DOVER ENGLAND - NIGHT

The DJ's goateed mouth speaks into a microphone.

ROBIN

Good evening children. You're listening to Outlaw Radio and I am the Bush Man. For those of you not totally baked, ring me with a request, Let's see what I can do.

CUT TO:

FULL SHOT - PETE'S CAR - DAY
Pete's car continues driving West on the interstate.

> MICK'S VOICE
> Hello, Bush Man?

> ROBIN'S VOICE
> (through the phone)
> Yes. What's your request?

> MICK'S VOICE
> How soon can you be in El Paso?

> ROBIN'S VOICE
> (through the phone)
> Who does that?

> MICK'S VOICE
> Robin, you dullard, it's me.

CUT TO:

INT. PIRATE RADIO STATION - DOVER ENGLAND - NIGHT
Robin talking on the phone.

> ROBIN
> Mick? So someone is listening!
> What was that song?

CUT TO:

INT. PETE AND MICK IN THE CAR - DAY
Mick talking on the cell phone.

>   MICK
> It's not a song. It's a request.
> (speaking slowly)
> How-soon-can-you-be-in-El Paso Texas?

>   ROBIN'S VOICE
> (through the phone)
> El Paso?

>   MICK
> Yes. We got a job. Unfinished business you know.
> Remember?

>   ROBIN'S VOICE
> (through the phone)
> You're not serious. Look, why are you out there hunting
> them down? You're with that Yank aren't you.

>   MICK
> I am and we're not. They came to us. If you want to do
> the right thing we really need your help. Can you come
> out? We'll fill you in when you get there.

CUT TO:

INT. PIRATE RADIO STATION - DOVER ENGLAND - NIGHT

Robin hangs up the phone and slowly spins around in his chair. He pauses, looking over at the girl. He slowly turns around thumbing through a stack of albums, pulls one out and puts it on the turntable, puts the needle on the first song. Steve Miller's Space Cowboy starts to play. He stands up and walks over to the girl, taking a coat off the chair. He leans over and kisses her on the forehead.

> ROBIN

Sonya.

> SONYA

Yes?

> ROBIN

Don't forget to feed Samson.

CUT TO:

FULL SHOT PETE AND MICK IN THE CAR - DAY

Their car is driving west on the highway. Steve Miller's Space Cowboy is playing on the radio.

FADE OUT:

FADE IN:

EXT. EL PASO INTERNATIONAL ARRIVALS TERMINAL - DAY

Mick and Pete are standing outside their car watching a crowd walking out of the terminal. Out of the crowd appears Robin wearing jeans ripped at the knees and a military short sleeve shirt. A carry on bag is slung over his shoulder. Mick smiles and holds a finger up. Pete, Mick and Robin open the car doors and get in.

CUT TO:

INT. PETE MICK AND ROBIN IN THE CAR DRIVING AWAY - DAY

> MICK
>
> So that's it in a nutshell.

> ROBIN
>
> Yeah but...the desert?
> Tombstone?

> PETE
>
> We're not making the rules from here on out partner.
> Then again, we don't have to operate by the old ones
> either.

> ROBIN
>
> No skyscrapers to toss anyone off of out there I
> suppose.

> MICK
>
> Hey, it wasn't us.

> PETE
>
> Unfortunately.

> ROBIN

I'm just saying. Say, can we stop at an electronics store? I'll need a few things. You know, my family said we had a great aunt that once lived out there. Maggie Erwin I think her name was.

Mick turns to Pete.

> MICK

Here we go.

CUT TO:

FULL SHOT - OK CAFE - TOMBSTONE - MORNING
Mick and Robin are sitting at a picnic table on the patio outside the OK Cafe on Allen Street. They are looking at the road map. An area is circled where they think Omar's ranch is. Men and women are walking around in period clothing, a stage coach rolls by. Pete walks to the table with three coffees. As he puts them on the table, there is yelling and an explosion of gunfire in front of them from the street. Pete throws the coffee and all three dive to the ground screaming at each other. The shooting stops. Through the smoke, Mick looks up to see a pair of cowboy boots facing him. Robin is under the table. Mick looks up at the cowboy, RON FOSTER. His hand is outstretched. People around them are laughing loudly. Pete is cursing. Ron helps Mick up.

> RON

This must be yawls fist day here. We're sorry about that.

Pete stands up and brushes himself off.

PETE

Well that was fucking fun.

Ron glances at Pete disapprovingly.

RON

Welcome to Tombstone fellas. Our next show is at two.
I guess you know those were blanks. Mind if I take a
seat?

MICK

No, not at all.

Mick looks under the table.

MICK

Robin, you alive? You can come out now.

Pete, angry and dusting himself off, goes back for more coffee.

RON

Really. We didn't mean to catch you off guard like that.

MICK

That's all right mate.
Hell of a show you got.

*Ron looks down at the map and sees the circled area but doesn't
say anything about it.*

RON

Where are you fellas staying?

MICK

Those cabins down the street.
We just got in last night.

Pete comes back and places coffee on the table.

RON

Sure. That's a nice place. It's quiet this time of year
though. Not too many tourists.

Ron stands up and pats Robin on the shoulder.

RON

You boys enjoy your stay here.   We'll see you around.

*Ron turns and walks down Allen street. He walks up to LYNN
SWAN, another period actor who was watching the three. Ron
and LYNN, facing each other, pull out their pistols and re- load.*

RON

Kinda nervous for a couple of tourists. Got a map with
the ranch circled on it. Let's keep an eye on them.

CUT TO:

EXT. PETE, MICK AND ROBIN IN PETE'S CAR - NIGHT

*Pete's car with headlights on approaches a dusty dirt road off an
empty highway. The car pulls in several yards, stops and the headlights go off. All three get out. Three doors slam shut. They open
the map on the hood of the car and look at it with a flashlight.*

PETE

About a quarter mile that way and a couple of hundred

yards up to the top of the hill. Wish we had guns.

> MICK

With real bullets.

All three start to walk down the road into the darkness.

CUT TO:

EXT. TOP OF SANDIA HILL - NIGHT

Mick, Pete and Robin, struggling, breathing heavy, helping each other to the top of the hill. Their clothes are torn, arms scratched. They look up.

CUT TO:

P.O.V. TOP OF SANDIA HILL - NIGHT

All three look down onto a large adobe ranch house lit up inside and out, several hundred yards away. Two pick up trucks are parked next to a large metal barn. A small twin engine aircraft is parked and tied down with lights shining on it, a 500 gallon fuel tank next to it. A mercury vapor light on a telephone pole shines down on barbed wire at the entrance of the compound.

> MICK

Well, that's it.   What do you think?

> ROBIN

Cameras are no problem. I'd like to get closer and see about putting audio in there too.

Robin slowly makes his way down the hill towards the ranch.

CUT TO:

EXT. TOP OF SANDIA HILL - NIGHT

Robin, breathing heavily, noisily makes his way back to Mick and Pete.

> ROBIN
> Come on now? You there? Oh, all right.

> MICK
> Well, how did it go?

> ROBIN
> Great. I got a good look. I can wire that place in a flash. Nobody heard me.

> VOICE IN THE DARK
> Hell, we heard you a mile away.

Mick, Pete and Robin turn around, startled, and see the silhouette of four men in the dark, standing immediately behind them. As Robin falls back, Mick head butts one, Pete leans in and swings at the shadows, knocking two of them to the ground.
Legs and fists come out of the dark, knocking Mick and Pete down. A scuffle ensues.

> MICK'S VOICE
> Robin, run!

A shotgun being racked is heard in the darkness.

> VOICE IN THE DARK
> Nobody's going anywhere. Let 'em up.

Mick and Pete stand up. Pete is holding his jaw. Mick helps up Robin. LYNN SWAN is a tall man in boots, jeans and a western work shirt. He walks out of the darkness. A .45 pistol hangs in a holster from his hip.

LYNN SWAN

You're trespassing on private property.

PETE

(angrily) Sorry. We didn't see your fucking name on the hill.

The other three armed men walk out of the darkness, surrounding the three. Two of the men are American Indians.

LYNN SWAN

You're not too smart. Mouthing off here alone in the middle of the desert.

MICK

Look. We're lost. We didn't...

PETE

So what. You gonna take us down there to your friends?

Lynn Swan looks around at his party.

LYNN SWAN

Not hardly. We thought they were friends of yours.

PETE

Bullshit. You heard everything we said.

LYNN SWAN

Fair enough.

He motions towards the ranch.

LYNN SWAN

But if you don't want them to hear you, I suggest we move out of here.

Mick and Pete look at each other.

MICK

(low voice) They're not police are they?

PETE

No.

MICK

They all have guns don't they?

PETE

Yeah.

Mick dusts of Robin.

MICK

With real bullets?

PETE

This time? Probably.

MICK

Well?

                              PETE
        Let's go find the car.

                                                    CUT TO:

EXT. PETE'S CAR - NIGHT
*Mick, Pete and Robin walk out of the brush to their car, followed
by Lynn and the three men, all on horseback. Lynn looks down
at them.*

                           LYNN SWAN
        You fellas' know how to get back to the cabin?

                              PETE
        (whispering to Mick) Son of a bitch.

                           LYNN SWAN
        Someone will be by your place tomorrow. As we like to
        say, don't leave town. Have a good evening. Oh. Keep
        an eye out for snakes.

*Robin jumps around looking at the ground. The cowboys trot off
into the darkness.*

                              PETE
        Let's go.

                                                    CUT TO:

INT. CABINS OUTSIDE OF TOMBSTONE - MORNING
Pete, Mick and Robin are getting dressed, unpacking luggage,

making coffee. The door to the cabin is open. The radio is on. A pile of electronics gear is laying on the couch.

CUT TO:

INT. CABINS - MORNING

Pete is sitting on the edge of the bed. Reaching into a bag, he pulls out a prescription bottle, opens it, takes out a pill and swallows it. Mick is in the kitchen. He pours a cup of coffee, opens a prescription medicine bottle, takes out two pills and swallows it. Robin rolls over reaching into his pants. He takes out a blister pack, pops out a pill and swallows it. Mick turns toward the door, sees two shadows on the floor, looks up and takes a step back. Ron and Lynn Swan are standing in the doorway. Pete and Robin look towards the door.

> RON
>
> Morn-in'. Are you going to invite us in?

> MICK
>
> Sure. Coffee?

Ron and Lynn walk in and take their cowboy hats off and sit at the table.

> RON
>
> No thanks.

Pete and Robin walk into the room.

> RON
>
> You city boys sure do make a lot of noise. Apart from us, do you have any idea what else has crept in here in the last twenty minutes?

Robin looks around the floor. shoulder.

> PETE

Enough already!

> RON

Pete slaps Robin on the

I heard ya'll had an interesting night last night.

> MICK

Yeah, that was nice of your mates to help a couple of lost tourists out of the desert.

> RON

Tourists. That ranch ya'll were scoping out last night isn't on the tourist map.

Ron points to the map.

> RON

But it's on yours.

> PETE

Look, we can bullshit all day, or you can tell us who you guys are.

> RON

Fair enough.

Ron pulls back his vest, revealing a badge.

                          RON

The men you ran into last night and I are Arizona
Territorial Rangers.

                         ROBIN

Rangers? Like Texas Rangers?

                      LYNN SWAN

Same church, different pew.

                          PETE

Yeah right. That tin is probably as real as those blanks
you're using.
When are they gonna give you guys real bullets?

Lynn starts to stand up. Ron motions him to sit down.

                          RON

I'll get to the point.

                          RON

We know ya'll aren't police. But I don't think you're
crooks either. So if you fellas don't want to talk to us,
I'd be more than happy to send over a couple of sheriff's
deputies and a state trooper or two. So what do you say.

Mick and Pete look at each other then back at Ron.

                          RON

We've been watching that ranch for some time now
and it's usually deader than road kill. It's not a working
ranch but activity has been picking up there in the last

few days. Then you boys show up. We think they're going to fly up a load of dope. Let me know when I'm getting warm.

Pete and Mick look at each other again and shrug.
Mick turns to Robin.

> MICK

Close the door.

CUT TO:

EXT. CABINS OUTSIDE OF TOMBSTONE - MORNING

The cabin door opens up. Everyone walks out and stand in a circle.
Ron and Lynn put their cowboy hats back on.

> RON

So you feel pretty sure that's what it is?

> PETE

Positive.

Ron looks around.

> RON

Well ya'll can't stay here. Go eat, come back and pack. I'll have someone come for you this afternoon. All right?

> MICK

Sure.
Thanks.

Everyone shakes hands. Ron and Lynn turn and walk towards the car when Ron turns around.

> RON
>
> We're sorry about your friends.
> Look, there's three things you need to survive out here.
> Boots, water and guns. You can get all that in town.

> PETE
>
> Ron.

> RON
>
> Yes sir?

> PETE
>
> You know, anything starts to smell and we'll shut it down.

> RON
>
> Well let's hope not.
> We'll see you in a little bit.

CUT TO:

EXT. ALLEN STREET, TOMBSTONE - DAY
Mick and Robin are walking down the sidewalk in new western wear and cowboy hats, carrying bags. As they walk up to a gun store, Pete walks out with two rifles and a heavy box with two pistols and ammunition.

PETE

Welcome to America fellas.

Pete hands a lever action rifle to Mick, who smiles.

MICK

Oh bloody right!

Robin turns to Mick, reaching out for the rifle.

MICK

Don't even think about it.

All three start walking down the sidewalk. Pete hears a metallic chinking sound, stops and turns around. He looks down at Robins boots and sees spurs.

PETE

Didn't take him long to go native did it. Let's get some water.

CUT TO:

EXT. RON'S RANCH - DAY

Ron and Lynn are standing on the covered wood deck porch in front of Ron's ranch house several miles outside of Tombstone. The ranch is surrounded in barbed wire fence. A large corrugated double door metal barn stands thirty yards from the house. They look out towards a dirt road with four men slowly approaching in the distance on horseback, kicking up a trail of dust. Lynn spits tobacco juice out into the dirt. Ron is smoking a cigarette.

LYNN SWAN

I don't know. I just don't trust 'em. Especially that smart one. There's more to that story.

RON

You're probably right. We'll give 'em a long leash for now.

Ron throws down the cigarette and steps on it.

RON

Make sure you tell the others.

Pete, Mick and Robin, led by an Indian, SAM, ride up to the porch on horseback and stop, luggage and bags are tied to the horses. Robin and Sam check out each other's pony tail. Everyone dismounts and walk up to Ron. Lynn walks off without acknowledging the group, gets into a pick up truck and leaves.

RON

Thanks Sam.
Ya'll enjoy the ride?

ROBIN

I couldn't find the A/C switch.

Sam leaves the group, riding by, looking down at Robin and shakes his head, annoyed.

ROBIN

Tell me, what was that balloon back there?

                    RON

Balloon? You mean blimp.
Well son, that's your problem.

                    PETE

It's a Border Patrol static observation platform. Long
range high resolution cameras and radio repeaters.

                    RON

And night vision. They operate it twenty four seven
looking for illegals. At that altitude it sees out about
sixty miles. Word is it can read a license plate at twenty
miles. Doesn't see through the mountains too good
though so there's a lot of blind spots. Get your gear and
come on in.

                    MICK

So it covers our ranch?

                    RON

I'm afraid it can.

                                                    CUT TO:

INT. RON'S LIVING ROOM - AFTERNOON
*Ron, Mick, Pete and Robin are standing around a large wooden
dining room table. The interior is rustic. Pete is drinking a beer.
Mick is holding the rifle. Electronic devices, coaxial cable, small
surveillance cameras, monitors, power cords and small solar panels
are spread all over the table.*

RON

Looks like ya'll cleaned out a few Radio Shacks.

ROBIN

And an electronic supply store or two.

RON

So what's your plan?

PETE

We wait until dark. Put the creep on the ranch, put
Robin in there and let him do his thing.

ROBIN

I can wire four rooms for sight and sound. Put a
repeater on top of that hill where your guys caught us
and relay the signal to the monitors here.

*The front door opens and two American Indian men walk in,
acknowledge Ron and take off their hats. Everyone turns towards
them. Ron nods to them and turns back to Robin.*

RON

Damn. Any chance they'll find any of this?

ROBIN

I haven't been caught yet.

PETE

What's the life expectancy on the batteries?

ROBIN

Eleven days. You see, it's a passive system. It's only pulling two mili amps of...

MICK

Ok ok ok, don't start.

RON

(smiling)
Fellas, this is BEN and his brother ROBERT. They'll take Robin to the ranch tonight. How does it look over there?

ROBERT

It's empty right now.

Ron looks out the window.

RON

Good. It'll be dark soon.
Let's start loading up.

CUT TO:

INT. RON'S LIVING ROOM - NIGHT
With Ron watching, Pete and Mick finish plugging in two camera monitors on the table, attaching a box antenna to both. Mick turns on the monitors, both screens are black.

MICK

Ron, how far are we from the ranch?

RON

About four miles. They should be there in a few
minutes.

*Mick picks up the lever action rifle again and works the lever,
making a loud cocking noise.*

MICK

God, I love that sound.

PETE

Are you gonna sleep with that thing or what?

RON

What did you do about the cabin?

Pete takes a sip from a can of beer.

PETE

I left it on the card.
The car is still there too.

Suddenly one of the monitors lights up, then the other.

MICK

OK, here we go.

*All three stand around the monitors. One monitor shows a wide
angle of a living room. The other monitor shows four smaller
screens, including an office, two bedrooms and a kitchen.*

PETE

That little friggin' hippie did it.

RON

I suppose it's too late to ask, but how much time are we looking at if those were found?

PETE

Federal? About twenty years a camera. Hey Ron, you wanted in. Now your in.

CUT TO:

INT. RON'S LIVING ROOM - DAY
Robin is sitting at the table watching the monitors. A pile of empty Dr. Pepper cans are stacked next to him. Lynn Swan is standing over Robin's shoulder watching. Mick and Ron are standing out on the porch. Pete walks into the room.

PETE

Anything?

ROBIN

Not yet. There's a guy in the living room and the fat man is in the study. Hold on, here we go.

CUT TO:

FULL SHOT MONITOR - DAY
Omar walks into his living room and hands the man a piece of paper.

OMAR

There's a duffle bag in the back of it. I need it by Friday.

Get the bag and bring it back here. Can you do that?

RANCH HAND
(heavy Spanish accent) Of course, no problem.

The ranch hand takes out a cell phone and makes a call. He begins to speak in Spanish, reading off the paper.

CUT TO:

INT. RON'S LIVING ROOM - DAY
Lynn suddenly reaches over Robins shoulder, knocking over a soda, and grabs a piece of paper and a pen. Watching the monitor, Lynn begins to write.

CUT TO:

FULL SHOT MONITOR - DAY

OMAR
Call me when you have it.

He looks at his cell phone.

OMAR
Here's my number.

CUT TO:

INT. RON'S LIVING ROOM - DAY
Lynn continues writing as Ron Mick and Sam walk in.

                    LYNN SWAN

Your boy just told that guy to pick up a bag at a truck
yard down in Mexico.

Lynn hands the paper to Pete.

                    LYNN SWAN

He wants it within forty eight hours.

                      PETE

Thanks.
Do you know where?

                    LYNN SWAN

I'm assuming down in Agua Prieta, across from
Douglas. That's the truck's number and your boy's cell
phone in case you want to call him. Russ and Tony are
down the road. We'll cold trail him if he goes across.

                      RON

Good job Lynn. Let us know.
Well, what now?

                      PETE

Robin can stay on the monitors.
Pete looks at the paper.

                      PETE

Mick and I need to go down to Bisbee. There's a guy
there we need to talk to.

LYNN SWAN

I knew it.

PETE

You knew what?

RON

I thought we were keeping this thing in house?

PETE

Who said we weren't? We're going to meet a guy to see what Customs knows. What, I gotta ask for fucking permission now? Besides, what do you care who gets it as long as the bad guys don't?

There is a pause as Ron and Pete stare at each other suspiciously.

PETE

C'mon Mick, let's go.

CUT TO:

INT. RON'S LIVING ROOM - MOMENTS LATER
Ron and Sam are left with Robin, sitting at the table watching the monitors.

RON

So I guess you've known those two for some time.

ROBIN

Yes.

For some time.

                              RON

Pretty good friends?

                            ROBIN

I'm here aren't I?

                              RON

Ha ha. I suppose you're right. I'm just not too sure
about them yet.

                                                    CUT TO:

P.O.V. COFFEE SHOP IN BISBEE -DAY
*Pete and Mick are standing in front of a coffee shop. A young
man in boots, pressed jeans and a dress shirt walks up and shakes
hands with Pete, then Mick. They walk into the shop and sit at
a table at the window. People walk down the sidewalk past the
window without noticing them. They lean into a huddle at the
table, speaking and gesturing amongst each other. Pete hands the
man a piece of paper.*

                          ROBIN'S VOICE

They're like a couple of old ghosts what found each
other. Spent their whole lives on this planet chasing
villains, and nobody in the real worlds ever seen 'em
doin' it. 'Cept maybe a few. It's all they know. Lost
their souls a long time ago and now they're tryingto get
them back. This is all they're good for. And except for

their signatures on some reports what's stashed away in a warehouse, nobody's ever going to know they were here, you know? But before you get to boo hooin', you need to know, they're not like us. Everybody wants to leave behind a grand legacy, a monument of some kind. They'll leave nothing more than the tail end of a breeze. I suppose that's their price.

RON'S VOICE

Price for what?

ROBIN'S VOICE

To see what nobody else sees.

All three stand up at the table, shake hands and leave.

CUT TO:

EXT. HILL OVERLOOKING CONTAINER YARD IN MEXICO - DAY

Lynn, Tony and Russel are standing next to their pick up trucks on a bluff in Douglas Arizona, overlooking a huge sixty acre container yard in Mexico. Braced against the truck, Lynn and Tony bring binoculars up to their faces.

CUT TO:

P.O.V. THROUGH BINOCULARS - DAY

Through binoculars, the ranch hand is seen standing next to his pick up truck parked next to a container in the far corner of the yard. Two other men are standing next to him talking and looking around. They open the back of a container, the doors obscure the inside. The ranch hand pulls out a dusty heavy duffel bag and lets it fall to the ground. He points his remote alarm key at his truck. The whole bed of the truck slowly raises up revealing a hidden compartment. With the help of one of the other men, they place the duffle bag in the compartment. The ranch hand closes the bed with the remote.

CUT TO:

INT. RON'S LIVING ROOM - AFTERNOON
Ron, Sam and Robin are sitting around the table. They hear car doors slam shut and the front door opens. Lynn walks in followed by Mick and Pete.

> RON

Well, any luck?

> LYNN SWAN

He took a duffle bag out of a
container. Is he back yet?

> ROBIN

No.
We haven't seen him.

> RON

How about you boys?

> PETE

Customs doesn't know anything but they're checking on
that number.

> RON

Well then, I guess we just wait.

Pete walks into the kitchen when his cell phone rings. He answers the phone.

CUT TO:

INT. CUSTOMS OFFICE IN DOUGLAS - AFTERNOON

Special Agent Keith Rogers is sitting in his office, in front of a computer terminal with a phone resting on his shoulder to his ear. Nervously chewing gum.

> KEITH ROGERS

Hey can you talk? That container number you gave me. Does it ring a bell? No? It should. That's your container.

CUT TO:

INT. PETE STANDING IN THE KITCHEN - AFTERNOON

Pete is on his phone looking into the group in the living room.

> PETE

(whispering) What the fuck are you talking about?

CUT TO:

INT. CUSTOMS OFFICE IN DOUGLAS - AFTERNOON

Keith is staring at the computer screen. Stops chewing his gum.

> KEITH ROGERS

That container. That's your container. From your case.

The one that got ripped in Houston way back.

CUT TO:

INT. PETE STANDING IN THE KITCHEN - AFTERNOON
Staring off into space, Pete turns pale.

PETE

Thanks. I'll call you.

Pete slowly closes the cell phone. He walks back into the living room.

ROBIN

So when I told Ron about my great Aunt Maggie living in Tombstone, he said to check out the Bird Cage.

PETE

Mick. That was Keith.

Everyone turns and looks at Pete.

PETE

It's not over.

MICK

That's our container isn't it.

PETE

Yeah.

                         RON
So I guess you boys were right after all.

                         PETE
That container holds enough military arms to take over
both sides of the border.

                       LYNN SWAN
What about the duffle bag?

                         PETE
If I'm right, it's holding eight hundred thousand of
Uncle Sam's money.

                       LYNN SWAN
    Lord.

                                              CUT TO:

INT. CUSTOMS OFFICE IN DOUGLAS - AFTERNOON
Keith Rogers picks up the phone and dials a number.

                      KEITH ROGERS
    Yeah boss. When are you coming back to the office? I
    really need to talk to you. OK.

                                              CUT TO:

EXT. PATIO BAR IN TOMBSTONE - DAY
Mick, Pete and Robin walk into a covered patio at a bar in

Tombstone. Keith Rogers is already seated alone drinking a beer. Pete and Mick sit down. Robin motions behind him and starts to walk away.

ROBIN

I'm going to go check something out.

PETE

You're sure it's the same one.

KEITH ROGERS

Hey, it's the number you gave me. It's still in the system. You ought to be glad I found it.

MICK

It's not bringing back happy memories.

KEITH ROGERS

We'll get with Mexican Customs and go take a look. It shouldn't take...

Two men dressed in slacks, dress shoes and shirts enter, looking around, then walk up to the table. Keith looks at them, pauses, then looks down at the table.

GRANT SUTHERLAND

Keith, how are you. Drinking on the job already? Tsk. Tsk. You mind if we sit down?

KEITH ROGERS

I didn't call them.

                            PETE

Aw Christ.

                      GRANT SUTHERLAND

Close. FBI.

Grant sticks his hand out to shake hands.

                      GRANT SUTHERLAND

Grant Sutherland.

Pete stares at Grant and doesn't shake his hand. Grant and his partner sit down across from Pete and Mick. Pete stares at Keith.

                      GRANT SUTHERLAND

Ah, yes. The proverbial sit-down.

                      GRANT SUTHERLAND

No. Keith didn't call us. His boss did. Something about some missing
cash. How much is it? Eight hundred thousand? Look, before this gets completely out of hand, here's the deal. We know about the cash in the container and Omar and his ranch. Don't worry about it getting lost again because we know when it's coming in. We have taps going up on all their phones, a man on the inside and SWAT on standby to take it off. Don't worry Keith, you're invited.

                            PETE

The fat man's working for you isn't he.

GRANT SUTHERLAND

It doesn't make him a bad person does it? We're just dancing with the devil.

MICK

You keep harping about the money. What about the weapons?

GRANT SUTHERLAND

What about them? They're long gone. Probably rusting in Somalia by now. Look, I'm not in the recovery business. Besides, a load of guns wouldn't have made the same splash as a load of cash now would it. You and your friend, Mick, right? You're retired? So go be retired. Enjoy your cabin, get drunk.

Grant leans forward and speaks in a low voice.

GRANT SUTHERLAND

Then get the fuck out of here.

Grant and the other agent both stand up to leave.

GRANT SUTHERLAND

Look, you've got my sympathy. I understand the headlines would have looked great reading how you got your lost load back and vindicated your dead buddies. Personally I don't give a shit.

Grant looks around.

GRANT SUTHERLAND

Instead, the headlines gonna read how agent

Sutherland, get's the money back and his transfer out of this god forsaken shit hole. Hey, first time, I asked you nice. Right?

MICK

The devil wouldn't lie.

CUT TO:

INT. HALLWAY IN THE BIRD CAGE SALOON - DAY

Robin wanders down the hallway past rows of old sepia photographs of the Bird Cage. He suddenly stops and stares at the photo of a young girl in period dress. As he studies the photo, she stares back at him. A label at the bottom of the photo identifies her as house entertainer and singer Maggie Erwin, his great aunt.

CUT TO:

INT. RON'S LIVING ROOM - EVENING

Ron, Lynn, Robin, Mick and Pete are gathered around the table. Sam and Tony walk in.

RON

Thanks for coming boys. Where's Russel?

SAM

He's out looking for a few head of cattle.

RON

Well. I guess it's time to shit or get off the pot. What do you want to do?

PETE

Sounds like Omar's gonna kill a few birds with one container. He gives up the cash for a pass from the FBI on the murders. I'm sure he put it all on Dragon. They help him smuggle the guns back into the U.S. Maybe they think there's nothing but the money in there anyway. They let him keep the load and he turns around and gives it to those two pumpkin chucking mutts from San Antonio, which the FBI may or may not take off later.

MICK

It's all about the money. Isn't it.

LYNN SWAN

I don't like it. I just assume we stay out of their way and pull up stakes. We got no dog in this fight.

PETE

No you don't. But you did jack us up on that hill. You did bring us in here. And you do have enough wiretap equipment on the table to get us all a hundred years each.

RON

I don't like it either. But with all the law running around out there now, we don't have much of a choice right now. So I guess we sit back and watch the show.

CUT TO:

INT. RON'S LIVING ROOM - NIGHT

Robin and Mick are sitting in front of the monitors bored. Mick yawns. Suddenly Robin sits up and stares at the monitor.

> MICK
>
> Anything good on the telly tonight?

> ROBIN
>
> OK boys. Omar's back.

Pete and Ron walk over and stand behind Robin.

CUT TO:

P.O.V. MONITOR - NIGHT

The door opens to Omar's ranch. Omar walks into the living room, stops and turns around. The Ranch hand follows, dragging the duffle bag with both hands.

> OMAR
>
> Give it here.

Omar takes the bag, dragging it, cursing, into his study, closing the door behind him, locking it. Everyone looks at the other split screen monitor and watch Omar pull on a door concealed in the wall where he shoves the duffle bag into it, then pushes the door closed.

> ROBIN
>
> I'll be damned.

MICK

Somebody's not going to like that.

Omar walks into the living room, stopping to lock the door to his study.

OMAR

I'm flying tonight. Call me when you bring the
container here.
Understand?

PETE

He's never around when it goes down.

FADE OUT:

FADE IN:

*The next day. The Border Patrol Regional Command Center.
Uniformed officers are manning rows of radio consoles. Radio
traffic is heard in the background. A console sits in front of a large
projection screen at the back of the room. Grant Sutherland and
another agent are standing behind two officers seated at the console.*

GRANT SUTHERLAND

OK, show me what this blimp can do.

CUT TO:

P.O.V. PROJECTION SCREEN - DAY
A camera mounted on the blimp slowly scans across the desert,

stopping south and zooming in to what appears to be an intersection busy with traffic.

OFFICER

OK. That's the port of entry at Douglas. The container lot is a half mile south of there.

The camera zooms out and starts to pan north.

OFFICER

That's highway 666 from Douglas that runs past your targets ranch.

GRANT SUTHERLAND

Six, six, six. That's appropriate.

The officer moves a cursor over the screen.

OFFICER

Most of the commercial traffic goes west on eighty but yours will go this way.

As the camera pans north, the highway disappears behind a mountain ridge.

GRANT SUTHERLAND

What about that ridge?

VOICE

Nothing I can do about that. There's nothing back there but road. We have units keeping an eye on it today.

Grant Sutherland holds a hand held radio up to his mouth.

GRANT SUTHERLAND

Vista two ten to team leader. Everything is in place. Stand by.

VOICE

(through the radio) Roger.

CUT TO:

EXT. U.S. SIDE DOUGLAS PORT OF ENTRY - DAY

Keith Rogers is parked in his car near the port of entry, watching a parade of containers driving through the port into the U.S. He looks at the numbers on the containers as they slowly drive by. He stares at one, then looks at a piece of paper, puts the mike to his mouth.

KEITH ROGERS

Vista two ten, alpha sixteen o four.

GRANT SUTHERLAND

(through the radio) Two ten. Go ahead.

KEITH ROGERS

The target's on our side and is heading your way.

GRANT SUTHERLAND

(through the radio) That's clear. Hold your location. I'll tell you when to proceed.

Keith gives the finger to the mike.

CUT TO:

INT. TRACTOR RIG CARRYING CONTAINER - MOMENTS LATER

The tractor is in a line of slowly moving truck traffic driving west on highway eighty. It approaches a sign for highway 666 and turns right onto the highway.

CUT TO:

EXT. HIGHWAY 666 - DAY

The tractor trailer rig drives down a long, straight empty two lane highway. Heat waves radiate from the road. The legs and back of a uniformed Border Patrol Officer standing on the highway, come into view. Traffic cones block the lane, a sign says CHECKPOINT, a small mobile home office bears a U.S. Border Patrol sign next to the door, on the side of the road, a trash can and picnic table is under a tarp seating two other Border Patrol Officers eating lunch. A box fan blows on them. The truck slows down behind a passenger car that is waved on, the truck is directed to the side of the road opposite the office where another tractor trailer is leaving. The air brakes sound as the driver is motioned by the officer to go over to the office.

CUT TO:

INT. CHECK POINT OFFICE - DAY

The driver exits the cab and shuffles towards the office door, passing papers tacked to a board at the bottom of the stairs, he enters and walks up to the counter. An officer is looking down, writing on a clip board. Border Patrol radio traffic is heard over a scanner. The officer looks up at the driver. A large window is seen next to the door showing the truck in the background.

> OFFICER

Scale sheet and manifest.

The driver hands the officer his paperwork. The officer starts to write on the clipboard. A second tractor trailer rig approaches and is stopped by an officer, blocking the view of the truck. Air brakes sound outside.

> OFFICER

Where are you coming from today?

> DRIVER

Trans-Rio shipping in Agua Prieta.

> OFFICER

And you're hauling?

> DRIVER

Tile.

> OFFICER

Destination?

> DRIVER

El Paso.

As the truck outside slowly drives off, the officer writes on the clipboard, initials the bottom of the drivers forms, stamps the forms and hands the papers back to the driver.

OFFICER

There you go. Drive careful.

The officer looks back down at his clipboard as the driver walks out, climbs into his tractor and drives off.

CUT TO:

INT. BORDER PATROL COMMAND CENTRE - DAY

Grant Sutherland, and another agent are looking over the shoulder of the officer seated at the console operating the blimp camera. They look up at the wide screen.

GRANT SUTHERLAND

Well where the hell is it?

OFFICER

Give it a minute. It'll come into view. Wait, here it comes.

Grant talks into a hand held radio.

GRANT SUTHERLAND

Team one, target is on the move. ETA is twenty mikes.

CUT TO:

INT. RON'S LIVING ROOM - DAY

Robin sits in front of the monitors on the hill watching the ranch. Suddenly the view is momentarily obscured by someone standing in front of the camera. He pans the camera to see the back of the ranch hand and two Mexicans. He turns on the audio. He sees the tractor trailer drive slowly onto the ranch below and approach the house. Suddenly a van rushes in and stops. FBI SWAT agents jump out surrounding the truck. A parade of cars with blue lights on the roofs are seen driving in, screeching to a halt, kicking up dust.

CUT TO:

EXT. SANDIA HILLTOP OVER RANCH - DAY

Mick and Pete are watching the raid through binoculars. Mick looks over at the ranch hand and the Mexicans watching from another hill. The rifle rests next to Mick.

> MICK
>
> They're still there. Looks like the ranch hand didn't make it out. I can take him from here.

> PETE
>
> So can I.
> Watch this.

Pete dials a number on his cell phone.

> PETE
>
> Yes ma'am. This is Pete Velletri. Could you have Keith Rogers call me right away? Yes, my number is 512-555-1544. Yes ma'am, it's urgent. Thank you.

> MICK
>
> Did you just give her the ranch hand's cell number?

Pete looks back through his binoculars.

PETE

This is gonna be good.

CUT TO:

INT. RON'S LIVING ROOM - DAY
Robin watches the ranch hand and the Mexicans. The Mexicans are angry, speaking Spanish, they grab the ranch hand by the arms. His cell phone rings. One of the Mexicans takes the phone out of the ranch hands pocket and looks at the number.

MEXICAN

U.S. government?

CUT TO:

INT. RON'S LIVING ROOM - DAY Robin watching the monitor.

ROBIN

U.S. government?

CUT TO:

EXT. HILLTOP OVER RANCH - DAY
Pete and Mick watch the Mexican hit the ranch hand in the head with the cell phone. He grabs his head. Pete and Mick turn their binoculars back to the truck. They watch FBI agents, guns drawn, break the seals and locks, opening the back of the container. The agents pause then look at each other. One agent reaches up carefully and starts to help down a young Hispanic girl holding a baby. Other Hispanics slowly spill out of the container.

                    PETE
Mick, what the hell?

                    MICK
Somebody got ripped off.
Again.

                                        CUT TO:

EXT. BACK OF THE CONTAINER - DAY
*The SWAT team leader is standing in front of the driver who is
handcuffed, kneeling in the dirt. The agent talks into the radio.*

                SWAT TEAM LEADER
Two ten that's correct. Illegals. About forty, including
children.
The driver says he drove direct from Agua Prieta. Made
one stop at a Border Patrol checkpoint.

                                        CUT TO:

EXT. HIGHWAY 666 - DAY
*Keith Rogers is slowly driving up the empty highway, staring off
into the distance. He continues driving, not noticing a picnic table,
traffic cones and an overturned trash barrel on the side of the road.
He looks quizzically in the rear view mirror.*

                                        CUT TO:

EXT. KEITH ROGERS CAR - CONTINUOUS
Keith's car stops. Back up lights come on and tires squeal as he

backs up to the table. He gets out of the car and walks to the table and trash can. A car from the opposite direction, with lights and siren on, approaches from the north, coming to a screeching halt in front of Keith's car. Grant Sutherland and another agent get out and run towards Keith.

GRANT SUTHERLAND

What the hell are you up to?

Keith reaches into the barrel and pulls out a U.S. Border Patrol shirt. The badge is missing. He pulls out several other Border Patrol shirts. He turns to Sutherland.

KEITH ROGERS

Looks like it's memo time Grant.

CUT TO:

EXT. RON'S RANCH - DAY

Pete and Mick ride to the rear of the ranch by horseback. They dismount, Mick with the rifle by his side, to find Ron and Lynn sitting on the porch. They look over to the barn in time to see the tractor and container inside as a ranch hand closes the doors. Mick and Pete turn, looking up to Ron. Lynn stands up. Everyone hears Mick cock the trigger to the rifle. Lynn slowly rests his hand on his pistol.

RON

Whoa, easy boys. You wanted the truck didn't you?

Ron throws Pete the keys.
Pete looks at them.

                    RON

There you go. I know what you're thinking right about
now.

                    MICK

I bet you don't.

Ron stands and walks to the edge of the porch.

                    RON

You wanted it, you got it. If we
had told you anything, it would have gone to hell in a
hand basket.

                    PETE

How's that?

                    RON

Too many people talkin'. Blimps and cameras all over
creation. Half the FBI is in town. You never had a
chance. So there it is. It's yours. You can drive it down
main street for all I care. But I suggest ya'll lay low with
it for a few days until things blow over. This is going to
get worse before it gets better.

                  LYNN SWAN

I won't wait for a thank you card.

*Mick de-cocks the hammer. Mick and Pete walk up to Ron and
Lynn. They pause, then extend their hands. Everyone shakes.*

MICK

You're crazier than a box of frogs.

PETE

Where's Robin?

LYNN SWAN

After the FBI cleared out, he and the Indian went down to Omar's ranch. I think they're going for the money.

Pete and Mick curse, jump back on the horses and ride off.

CUT TO:

EXT. OMAR'S RANCH - AFTERNOON

Robin and Larry are looking through an open rear window into the living room. A fan inside is on full, blowing out the window. They see the ranch hand tied to a chair, his shirt is off. Duct tape is wrapped around his mouth and eyes. His head is taped by his neck to the high backed chair. A Mexican takes two bottles of motor oil, unscrews the tops and throws them on the floor. He slowly empties the bottles over the ranch hand, thick oil cascades over his head and shoulders. The second Mexican laughs as the ranch hand tries to recoil in the chair, breathing quickly through his nose.

The first Mexican lights a hand held propane torch. He waves the long lazy yellow flame under the ranch hand's chin, singing it. The ranch hand tries to jump back in the chair. The Mexican twists the knob, turning the flame blue. The flame starts to hiss. Hearing it, the ranch hand tries to scream, clear mucus blows through his nose.

CUT TO:

EXT. OMAR'S RANCH - AFTERNOON

Robin drops below the window and starts to hyperventilate.
Larry calmly covers Robin's mouth with his hand, whispering.

LARRY

Make a sound and we'll be in there with him.

A blood curdling scream roars through the window, followed by
high pitched squeals of laughter and stomping. The fan starts to
blow black smoke out the window.

CUT TO:

EXT. HILLTOP OVER RANCH - AFTERNOON

Mick and Pete are watching Omar's ranch through binoculars. The
ranch appears quiet. Suddenly a small twin engine plane flies just
feet over them. Pete and Mick watch it land and taxi to the ranch.
Moments later, a dark suburban races to the front of the ranch.
Two Mexicans get out, grab Omar and walk him into the house.

CUT TO:

INT. OMAR'S RANCH - AFTERNOON

The Mexicans push Omar into the smoke filled living room. Omar
recoils at the sight of the ranch hand and the men.

MEXICAN

Get it.

Omar turns and is followed into his office. He opens the safe behind
the false wall and looks down. The duffle bag is gone.

OMAR

OK. OK. My ranch hand must have taken it!

The Mexican looks over at the ranch hand's smouldering body. A charred stump is all that is left of his head.

MEXICAN

No my friend. I don't think so.

The Mexicans curse in Spanish, throwing Omar, screaming, into the safe. They lock the door and leave the room.

CUT TO:

EXT. HILLTOP OVER RANCH - AFTERNOON

Pete and Mick watch as all four Mexicans walk out of the house. The last one stops at the door. He lights several road flares and throws them into the house. He closes the door. All four get into the Suburban and drive off. The house quickly starts to burn.

PETE

Oh Jesus.

Pete and Mick race down the hill on horseback to the house. Yelling Robin's name, they run up to the door but it is engulfed in flames. The horses rear up and back away. Pete runs around the back as Mick throws a chair through a front window. Smoke billows out.

MICK

Oh Christ no!

Pete reappears through the smoke with Robin and Larry. Robin is dragging the duffle bag. They all get on the two horses, Robin carrying the duffle bag, and ride off.

CUT TO:

INT. RON'S LIVING ROOM - AFTERNOON

Ron and Lynn are standing in the living room. The front door opens, Mick, Pete, Larry and Robin, still carrying the duffle bag, enter. Robin, smiling, drops the bag in the middle of the floor.

RON

Well, welcome home boys.

Mick turns to Robin and punches him in the face, knocking Robin over a table. Pete and Larry grab Mick.

MICK

Think you're a smart guy do you! You fucking dullard! You fucking prat! What the hell were you thinking!

Robin pulls himself up, holding his jaw.
Pete and Larry pull Mick away from Robin.

ROBIN

I saw the combination on the tele! I knew you couldn't get there in time, so I went ahead and nicked it!

RON

All right. That's enough. You boys have some new problems for now. The FBI and Border Patrol are out there looking for that truck, and you. And we heard they're bringing more agents in tomorrow. They've closed the port and your friend at Customs is getting jammed up pretty bad right now. I'm surprised they haven't been here already. I think it's time we went our separate ways.

                    PETE

What about all this gear?

                    RON

We'll take care of it.

                    MICK

And the rest? We came a long way for it.

                    RON

We know. It's not going anywhere.
I wish I could tell you we had a use for it but we don't.

Mick points to the duffle gab.

                    MICK

And that?

                    RON

Too much blood on it for my taste son.

                    LARRY

It's cursed.

*Pete takes Ron to a corner of the room and puts the keys to the
truck into Ron's hand. Pete whispers to Ron.*

                    PETE

One last favour?

                    RON

I'll call you when it's done.

                    193

CUT TO:

INT. CRYSTAL PALACE - TOMBSTONE - EVENING

The bar is crowded and very noisy. Patrons are cheering and laughing. Mick, Pete and Robin are sitting at a table holding their drinks. Mick is on a cell phone. Pete looks serious and drained. Robin is enjoying the scenery. Flogging Molly is playing; 'If I Ever Get Out Of This Place Alive'. Mick hangs up his cell phone. Pete leans into Mick.

PETE

Well, what did she say?

MICK

Meeting me up in Benson at the bus station.

All three click their glasses together and laugh.

MICK

Cheers mate.
How about you?

PETE

I've had enough of the desert.   I'm gonna try
something different.
Sorry we didn't make it to Vegas.

MICK

Speak for yourself.
How about him?

Pete throws a wadded up napkin at Robin, trying to blow his nose, but his jaw hurts.

ROBIN

Do what?

MICK

How about you Muppet? Where to from here?

ROBIN

Oh.
I'm staying.

MICK

You're not serious.

ROBIN

I am. I had family here.
It kind
of feels like home now.

CUT TO:

INT. CUSTOMS OFFICE IN BISBEE - MORNING
Keith Rogers follows his boss towards the front door. As they pass, the secretary holds up a stack of paperwork. Keith takes the pile with both hands and places them under an arm.

SECRETARY

Keith, can you drop that off at the Regional office?
Thanks Hun. Good luck at the meeting. Oh, that
envelope on top is for you.

CUT TO:

EXT. PARKING LOT - MORNING
Keith and his boss walk towards an SUV.

> SUPERVISOR

I don't know.

> SUPERVISOR

I'm in the KMA club so there's not much they can do to me. I don't think they'll try to file criminal on you, but if you keep your job, I'm pretty sure you can kiss this place goodbye.

> KEITH ROGERS

And go where?

Keith and his boss reach the SUV and open the doors. The supervisor looks over the roof.

> SUPERVISOR

Where indeed. Well. I wouldn't expect anything better than Bisbee.

CUT TO:

INT. SUV - MORNING
Both men are driving down the highway. Keith is staring out into the distance. Neither are talking. He looks down at the stack of papers in his lap and sees the Fed Ex package addressed to him. He opens it. A set of truck keys and a business card falls out. Keith reads the business card.

> KEITH ROGERS

Clover Trucking.

> SUPERVISOR

What about it?

Keith looks at his boss and holds up the truck keys.

CUT TO:

EXT. BUS STOP IN BENSON - DAY

Mick leans against Pete's car, parked next to the gas pumps at a convenience store. A Greyhound bus approaches from the east and rolls to a stop. The driver and several passengers get out, walking into the store.

> DRIVER

Ten minutes folks.

A minute passes. Mick turns towards Pete.
Pete shrugs. Behind him, Mick hears Jodie's voice.

> JODIE

Hey cowboy! Did you ever find your bridge?

Mick and Jodie walk up to each other, stopping just feet apart.
Pete gets out of the car holding Mick's suitcase.

> MICK

I wasn't sure.

> JODIE

Well you mentioned Vegas, I figured you could use

some luck.

> MICK

Which is already changing for the better.

Mick kisses Jodie and turns to Pete and takes the suitcase. They shake hands.

> PETE

So. Give me a call. Save enough to get home. And don't wear your spurs to bed.

> MICK

Ha Ha. Cheers mate.

CUT TO:

EXT. CLOVER TRUCKING - DAY
An SUV drives slowly down a row of parked tractor trailer rigs in a huge truck yard, kicking up dust. The SUV comes to a halt, then backs up.

> KEITH ROGERS

That's it.

> SUPERVISOR

Are you sure?

Both men get out of the SUV. Keith approaches the rear of a container, breaking the seals with a screwdriver.

                    SUPERVISOR
        I hope you're right.

                    KEITH ROGERS
        (sarcastically) Yeah, I wouldn't want to get in trouble.

Keith puts the key from the envelope into the pad lock, pauses and turns it. The lock pops open. Keith looks at his supervisor. They both draw pistols.

                                                    CUT TO:

P.O.V. CLOVER TRUCKING - DAY
Keith swings open the container doors, revealing dusty cases. the container of weapons and ammunition stacked all the way to the rear. Keith pulls a heavy duffle bag from the floor of dropping it onto the dusty ground and opens it. Bundles of neatly wrapped U.S. currency are stacked inside. Keith holds up a bundle to his supervisor.

                    SUPERVISOR
        Forget what I said about Anchorage.

                                                    CUT TO:

INT. LAS VEGAS CASINO - DAY
Mick is standing away from a crowd, watching Jodie throwing a winning dice at a craps table, to the cheers of the other players. He pulls out a cell phone and makes a call.

CUT TO:

EXT. PETE AT THE HELM OF A HOUSE BOAT - DAY

Pete, in shorts and a tank top, is at the wheel, docked in a marina, starting the engines and turning on radios. His cell phone rings. He looks at the number and answers.

                          PETE

   Hello?

CUT TO:

INT. LAS VEGAS CASINO - DAY

Mick talking on his cell phone.

                          MICK
   So, did they ever pay out for that thing in Laredo?

CUT TO:

EXT. PETE AT THE HELM OF A HOUSE BOAT - DAY

Pete, talking on the phone, continues to turn on electronics.

                          PETE

   I'm standing on my half.
   Tell me you didn't get married.

CUT TO:

INT. LAS VEGAS CASINO - DAY

Mick talking on the cell phone.

MICK

C'mon mate. You know I wouldn't push my luck out here.

CUT TO:

EXT. PETE AT THE HELM OF A HOUSE BOAT - DAY
Pete sits in the captains chair.

PETE

Can you meet me in Key West in a month? I'm holding your share.

CUT TO:

INT. LAS VEGAS CASINO - DAY
Mick smiles, looks at the floor.

MICK

We can do that. See you in a few weeks. Be safe.

Mick hangs up the phone. He looks at Jodie at the craps table. She looks up at Mick with a big smile and holds up her hand, showing a wedding ring.

CUT TO:

EXT. PETE AT THE HELM OF A HOUSE BOAT - DAY
Pete lights a cigar, puts the boat in gear, and idles out of the marina. Holding the throttle, he looks out, smiles and murmurs to himself.

PETE

It'll end in tears.

The boat idles out of the marina showing the name of the boat on the stern: 'Serendipity'.

FADE OUT:

THE END